Born in Malaysia and fluent in both Mandarin and Cantonese, Tony Tan trained at La Varenne, France, and Leiths School of Food and Wine in the UK. He has presented master classes and been guest chef at hotels and restaurants throughout Australia, China, Malaysia, Vietnam, New Zealand and Spain, including the Ritz in Madrid and Alambique, one of Spain's top cooking schools. He was an international judge at Hong Kong's premier Chinese cuisine challenge, The Best of the Best Culinary Competition. He writes for magazines and newspapers in Australia and internationally and comments regularly in the media on food and wine.

HONG KONG FOOD CITY

HONG KONG FOOD CITY

tony tan

MURDOCH BOOKS
SYDNEY · LONDON

contents

what an exciting book!

There can be no better guide to the glories of eating in Hong Kong than Tony Tan. Tony is known to many as an exceptionally talented cook; now he reveals himself as a fine writer and one who truly understands his subject. He is interested in history and tradition as well as flavour. Tony is a cook's cook. He never takes shortcuts; he explains and he reveals the full story. It helps that he is a fluent Cantonese and Mandarin speaker and as he jokes and banters with the stall holders at street food stands and markets, or the chefs of starred restaurants, you just know he is gathering insight and registering detail.

The recipes in this book include the very modern along with the traditional. There has been no watering-down of technique to please a Western reader. Rather, Tony has included meticulous explanations of Chinese ingredients and methods. Some of the recipes are challenging and almost certainly will require that the interested cook makes several visits to Chinatown to search out unknown ingredients. Which all just adds to the fun.

Anyone planning a trip to Hong Kong can follow Tony's recommendations to his favourite spots, ranging from the humble *dai pai dong* to the Michelin-starred Amber restaurant.

The photography is marvellous; not just Greg Elms' images of mouth-watering food, but also the atmospheric street scenes of Hong Kong and its people by Earl Carter.

STEPHANIE ALEXANDER

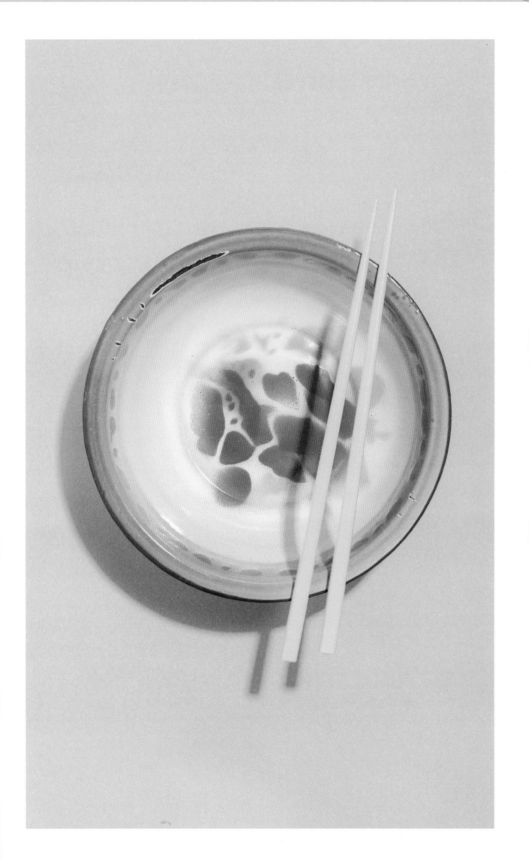

a brief history of Hong Kong

YOU CAN ALMOST FEEL THE RUSH OF PEOPLE IN HONG KONG, A CITY THAT SEEMS TO BE CHARGING ALONG IN OVERDRIVE. IT IS SPECTACULAR IN MANY WAYS.

A mere dot on the map, Hong Kong is one of the world's top five financial centres, its glittering skyscrapers are a sight to behold and its renowned shopping centres cater to just about every whim and fancy. Bilingual and confident, on the arts front it is the envy of many Asian cities, and its food scene is truly a food lover's paradise. But Hong Kong was not like this less than two hundred years ago.

Hong Kong was built on power and colonisation. Hong Kong Island was ceded to the British by China's weak Qing emperors in 1842. A subsequent war resulted in China also ceding Kowloon and Stonecutter's Island in 1860. In 1898, fearing their fledgling colony could not defend itself unless they also controlled the areas north of Kowloon, the British negotiated a 99-year lease of the New Territories. Sovereignty reverted to China in 1997 when that lease ended.

During this 99-year period, Hong Kong's population grew exponentially. The colony enjoyed a stable political environment amid the chaos existing in mainland China, brought on by internal strife and encroachments by Japan and Western powers. In the decades leading up to the First World War, Hong Kong developed into an entrepôt for Chinese trade, with mercantile companies such as Jardine Matheson playing a major role. Meanwhile, the Qing dynasty was toppled by Dr Sun Yat Sen and, for a time, warlords ruled much of China. More refugees arrived in Hong Kong.

In the years approaching the handover in 1997, Hong Kong's free-trade status saw its economy grow steadily. However, it was not always smooth sailing. Despite the British laissez-faire attitude, continued political turmoil in China had an impact. Hong Kong's lowest point was the Japanese occupation from 1941 to 1945, which led to much hardship and forced evacuation to China. But Hong Kong's fortunes changed with the Chinese civil war between the Communists and Nationalists. The 1949 Communist takeover led to another massive influx of refugees, both rich and poor. Affluent businessmen and tycoons from Shanghai set up labour-intensive industries in their new home, including textile and plastic toy manufacturing. This shift to manufacturing proved to be the saviour of Hong Kong's battered economy.

By the 1960s, with industrialisation and trade spearheading the way, Hong Kong's economy boomed and the city's food changed with it, although there were curious anomalies in the early days. The tastes of the British establishment meant that gammon, roast beef, tinned oatmeal and claret often graced the table. Life revolved around tennis, cricket, clubs, afternoon teas and drinks in classy hotels such as the Peninsula, which opened in the late 1920s. The British viewed the food of the Chinese with suspicion – perhaps due to chauvinism or simply an inability to adapt to local tastes.

The Chinese, on the other hand, bound by colonial policies and restrictions, stuck to their teahouses, street stalls, markets and burgeoning restaurants to the west of the island in Sheung Wan and Sai Ying Pun. They also enjoyed Western foods in restaurants opened by their compatriots during the late 19th century. One of these is Tai Ping Koon restaurant. Featuring Western classics with a dash of Cantonese flair, these places came to be known as 'Soy Sauce Western' restaurants. The use of Worcestershire sauce in Cantonese cooking could have started in that period. Full of fascinating flavours, the cross-cultural offerings included 'Swiss' chicken wings, smoked pomfret and a giant soufflé that still captivates all who dine there today.

With new-found wealth, people ate out more and different eateries emerged. The city's predominantly Chinese population was obsessed with food, and had an innate sense of appreciation for it, stemming from thousands of years of culinary evolution based on yin-yang principles, creativity and regional variations. Hong Kong's Chinese food scene was extraordinary even in the late 1950s and early '60s.

Dai pai dongs, meaning 'big licence stalls', were created by the colonial administration to help families of injured or deceased civil servants after World War Two. They joined the throng of hawker stalls, serving anything from comforting congee to restaurant-quality food. Springing up everywhere from alleyways to under trees, these alfresco eating spots quickly became crowd favourites. However, over the years, complaints about noise and hygiene have forced large numbers of them into government-run food centres. Some, such as the ever-popular Leaf Dessert and Sing Heung Yuen in Central, are still operating street side. Tung Po, made famous by Anthony Bourdain, in North Point's wet market is one of the best *dai pai dong* experiences.

Another interesting development during this period was the blossoming of *cha chaan tengs* or Chinese cafés. Quite likely born from the British

tradition of drinking tea with milk, these catered for a dining public who were eager to taste Western food at affordable prices. Menus included variations on British food such as scrambled eggs, baked beans, prawn toast, macaroni, Spam omelette and a kind of calorific but delicious French toast with condensed milk and peanut butter. Some had bakeries that created iconic treats, such as egg tarts, 'pineapple' and 'cocktail' buns. Honolulu Café and Capital Café in Wan Chai are fine examples of this genre.

While you might not want to visit Hong Kong for baked beans and scrambled eggs, these neighbourhood eateries are expressions of what is unique about the city. What's even more interesting is the mind-boggling range of Chinese cooking styles on offer: from Cantonese to Sichuan to northern Chinese, this city has nurtured and cosseted the breadth and depth of Chinese food.

With Hong Kong bordering Guangdong province, Cantonese cooking naturally dominates. Revered throughout China, Cantonese belongs to the country's club of eight major cuisines. In fact, there's a saying in China that the best dining comes from Guangzhou (anglicised to Canton), the ancient city where most Cantonese people come from. This cooking style emphasises freshness and subtle seasoning that does not overwhelm the main ingredient. Cantonese cooks are masters of dim sum, the dazzling array of steamed buns and dumplings eaten in yum cha palaces and the elegant dining rooms of Hong Kong. Technically, Cantonese cooks are masters of the wok and famed for their ability to achieve the wok fragrance (*wok hei*).

Chiu Chow, also known as Chaozhou or Teochew cooking, comes from the group of Chinese people who speak a

Min dialect similar to the Hokkien people. Their ancestral home is in eastern Guangdong and their cuisine is often described as 'hearty'. They are best known for seafood dishes such as oyster omelette and cold crab, and long-simmered dishes such as braised goose, also pickles and dipping sauces made with tangerine and fish sauce. They love vegetables, fresh and preserved, and eat them in myriad forms. Chiu Chow cuisine also places an unusual emphasis on desserts.

Sichuan cooking, best known for its *ma la* (numbing and hot) flavours, is also a member of the club of eight major cuisines. Sichuan cooks' ability to combine hot, sweet, bitter, pungent, salty and sour flavours in a single dish has no parallel; this prowess is displayed in ma po doufu and kung pao chicken. That said, not all Sichuan food is hot – tea-smoked duck is one of the most beautiful, complex dishes from this land-locked province in western China.

Grouped together under the Beijing label commonly known as Jing Chai, Chinese food from northern China embraces Henan, Hebei, Shanxi and Shandong provinces. Of these, Shandong cooking, also called Lu cuisine, is the best known. Of the dishes from the north, the most famous are Peking duck, wheat-based breads and noodles, and the hotpot called *da bin lou*. Lamb is also very popular, especially among the minority Muslim–Chinese called the Hui. Restaurants that serve halal food in Hong Kong often display Arabic script on the shopfront.

The Hakka, or 'guest' people, settled in the walled villages of the New Territories centuries ago. The cuisine of this resilient farming community is shaped by the land. Salt is important to their diet, as are vegetables – both fresh and salted. Dishes such as salt-baked chicken and pork belly with preserved vegetables are Hakka classics. Once popular, Hakka restaurants went out of fashion, although health-conscious diners have now rediscovered this earthy cuisine and there's a resurgence of this cooking style.

Hong Kong today is a fascinating mix of East and West. Looking like a Manhattan rising from the South China Sea, this is a city where diversity mixes with ease. Fast paced and energetic, China's Special Administrative Region brims with youthful confidence. There are top-class hotels, wine bars and restaurants of every shade to fit your wallet. While it's undeniable that Hong Kong is a quintessentially Chinese city with temples and noodle shops, it is also tempered by its British legacy and sensibilities. After all, afternoon tea of cucumber sandwiches and scones with jam and cream are still de rigueur at the Peninsula, the grande dame of Hong Kong's hotels. And curry tiffin is as much a part of the city life as dim sum.

It's no secret that I'm in love with Hong Kong and its extraordinary food culture. Every time I return to visit my family, I am surprised by the ever-changing face of this metropolis. Cosmopolitan and urbane, Hongkongers embrace French, Italian and Spanish foods with gusto. Western chefs, such as Richard Ekkebus (Amber) and Shane Osborn (Arcane), along with local stars like Jereme Leung (Bo Innovation), Jowett Yu (Ho Lee Fook) and May Chow (Little Bao), continue to excite and inspire. I hope this collection of recipes will illuminate the rich culinary mélange of this gastronomic wonderland. While one eye focuses on the future, the other looks back on a rich heritage. Hong Kong is cool!

Hong Kong pantry

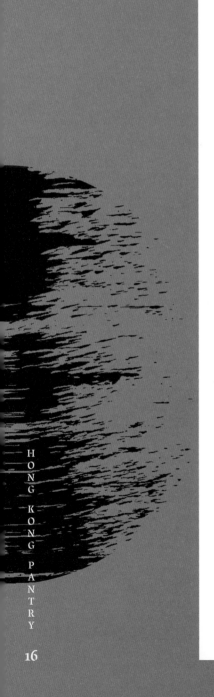

HONG KONG IS A VAST EMPORIUM OF INGREDIENTS FROM ALL OVER THE WORLD.

I've included the Chinese names for some – the first transliteration in Mandarin, which is widely spoken in Hong Kong, followed by Cantonese.

Almonds (*xing ren, hang yen*)
Chinese almonds are not true almonds but rather kernels of various varieties of the apricot family. Some are similar in flavour to bitter almonds and, like bitter almonds, they're mildly toxic and shouldn't be eaten raw. They're sometimes called northern almonds, and the sweeter varieties are known as southern almonds. Substitute regular almonds if they're not available.

Anchovies, dried
(*jiang yu zi, kong yu chai*)
Sun-dried anchovies are prized by the Chinese for their umami flavour and texture. These are found in most Asian supermarkets in Western countries. They're used in stock and stir-fried dishes.

Bamboo shoots (*zhu sun, jook soon*)
Fresh bamboo shoots are readily available in Asia but less so in the West. They must be peeled and boiled to remove their toxicity. Shoots canned in water are good, and most Chinese cooks blanch them before cooking. They add crunch and texture to spring rolls and stir-fried dishes.

Bean curd/tofu (*doufu, daofu*)
Best known as tofu in the West, bean curd comes in varying degrees of firmness – from custard-like to firm to extra-firm. Soft tofu is best for desserts and soups. Firm tofu is used in dishes such as ma po doufu. Extra-firm tofu is excellent in stews or deep-fried. Tofu flavoured with Chinese five-spice and soy sauce is great in stir-fries.

Dried bean curd or tofu sticks are made from the layers of skin that form on heated soy milk. They're perfect for braised dishes. Dried tofu skin is excellent for wrapping spring rolls. These are both found in the dried-goods section of Chinese supermarkets.

To make preserved tofu, also known as tofu cheese or fermented tofu, cubes of tofu are inoculated with a mould and fermented in jars with a solution of salt, rice wine and flavourings. White fermented tofu is eaten with congee and used in stir-fries. The red version, made with red yeast rice or red koji rice, is used in roast pork and braised dishes.

Black beans, fermented
(*duo zhi, dau si*)
Also called salted beans, these pungent soy beans are used to enhance the flavour of many dishes. They have been cooked, then sun-dried with salt and sometimes ginger. Rinse before use.

Black cardamom (*tsao kuo, cho ko*)
Black cardamom is not to be confused with green cardamom, although both are members of the ginger family. The smoky dried black pods are used in master stock. Crush lightly before use. At a pinch, substitute green cardamom, but the result won't taste quite the same.

Bok choy (*bai cai, baak choi*)
There are two varieties of bok choy: one has white stems and green leaves, and the other, known as Shanghai bok choy, is all green. The two varieties are interchangeable.

Celtuce (*qin wo, wo sun*)
Also called stem or asparagus lettuce,
this vegetable is cultivated more for its
crunchy stalks than its floppy leaves. The
leaves are seen in stir-fries and soups,
while the stalks are dressed with sesame
oil and rice vinegar as an appetiser. Use
broccoli stems if celtuce isn't available,
but peel the woody stalks first.

**Chilli bean paste
(*doubanjiang, daubanjeong*)**
Made from fermented chillies and
dried broad beans, this seasoning
is indispensable in Sichuan cooking.
The chilli bean pastes from Pixian in
Sichuan province are the most authentic.

Chilli oil (*la jiao you, laat chew yeaw*)
Sometimes used as a dipping sauce, chilli
oil is made by steeping chilli flakes in oil.
Homemade chilli oil is far superior to
shop-bought. (See recipe page 244.)

**Chilli sauce (*la jiao jiang,
laat ziu jeong*)**
Made with rice vinegar and sweet
potato, chilli sauce is the preferred
dipping sauce for dim sum. It's readily
available, but sriracha chilli sauce is a
good substitute. Koon Yick Wah Kee is
the cult chilli sauce in Hong Kong.

Chinese bacon (*la rou, lup yok*)
Flavoured with soy sauce, spices and
sometimes rice wine, this air-dried pork
belly lends a smoky fragrance to braised
and steamed dishes. It's delicious in
claypot rice. Look for it in Chinese
butchers and Asian supermarkets.

**Chinese five-spice
(*wu xiang fen, ng hiong fun*)**
A good five-spice is fragrant, sweet and
spicy. Blends, usually of cassia bark, star
anise, cloves, Sichuan peppercorns and
fennel, tend to vary. Avoid any that
smell musty.

Chinese ham (*huo tui, fo toi*)
This dry-cured ham from Yunnan
province and Jinhua has been much
lauded since Tang dynasty days.
It's used as a cold cut, in stews and
in stocks. Chinese ham is not sold in
the West, but jamón or prosciutto are
both good substitutes.

**Chinese red dates
(*hong zao, hong zou*)**
Native to China, this fruit, also known
as jujube, is crisp when fresh, but most
cooks prefer the dried variety to lend a
sweet note to soups, steamed dishes and
stews. It's also used in many desserts.
Regular dates aren't a substitute.

Chinese rice wine (*mi jiu, mai zau*)
Chinese wine falls into two categories:
clear like sake, and amber-coloured.
Both are made with glutinous rice and
a type of yeast. The clear variety, called
mi jiu, is used as a drink and a cooking
wine. The amber-coloured variety,
known as *huang jiu*, or yellow wine,
is named after the city of Shaoxing.
It gets its colour from the red rice yeast
used in the fermentation. There are
several grades of Shaoxing rice wine;
the best are reminiscent of a dry sherry.
Some are harsh and often labelled as
cooking wine. Avoid these and look for
the one with a pagoda on the label.
Manzanilla sherry is a good substitute.

**Chinese sausages
(*la chang, lap cheong*)**
Called 'wax sausages' thanks to their
texture, lap cheong sausages are made
with a mixture of lean and fatty pork,
or duck liver and pork. Highly aromatic,
lap cheong can be steamed or fried.

Chinese vinegar (*cu, chou*)
Chinese vinegars are generally made
from glutinous rice, although some are
made from sorghum, wheat and millet.

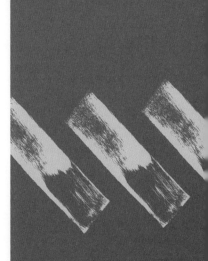

Most Asian grocers carry three varieties: clear, red and brown. Less harsh than Western versions, these range from strong and spicy to mild and sweet. They're used as dips, in stir-fries and for making pickles. Chinkiang vinegar, a black variety, is reminiscent of balsamic vinegar.

Daikon (*bai luo bo, bak lo baak*)
Also called Japanese or Chinese white radish, daikon radish resembles a large white carrot. It tastes like a mild red radish when raw, becoming more mellow when cooked. It's used in many dishes, such as radish cakes and stews, and is available year round.

Garlic chives (*jiu chai, gow choy*)
More pungent than regular chives, these flat chives are used in dumplings, seafood and egg dishes.

Ginger (*jiang, kiong*)
Like garlic, ginger is indispensable in Chinese cooking. In Asia, old ginger is preferred for cooking; young ginger is used for pickles. Look for ginger that's firm and smooth. Sand ginger (*Kaempferia galanga*) is a tiny rhizome that looks like ginger and has a peppery flavour; it's invaluable in certain sauces and Cantonese and Hakka dishes. It's also sold dried.

Goji berries (*gou qi zi, gai ji*)
These tiny reddish berries are from the matrimony vine, *Lycium barbarum*. Also called wolfberries, they taste like a cranberry with a tangy note. They're sold dried and are used in tonic soups, desserts and herbal teas.

**Hoisin sauce
(*hai xian jiang, hoi sin jeong*)**
Although the Chinese name suggests this sauce contains seafood, it doesn't. Made from fermented soy beans, wheat flour, garlic, vinegar, sugar and spices, this versatile thick brown sauce is great for stir-fries and marinating meats. It's also used as a dip for Peking duck, if sweet bean sauce, which is similar, isn't available.

Mushrooms (*gu, ku*)
Mushrooms hold a special place in Chinese cooking. Some, such as shiitake mushrooms, are loved for their intense flavour, and some, like cloud ear and wood ear fungus, for their crunchy texture. Most are sold dried or tinned. Apart from silver ear fungus, which appears mostly in sweet dishes, they're used in stir-fries and stews.

Mustard greens (*jie cai, gai choy*)
This member of the cabbage family comes in different forms, so shopping for it can be confusing. All have broad green leaves with a distinctive mustard flavour. One has closed bulbous stems and is usually pickled, preserved and brined. Another variety, called *mei cai* or *mui choy*, is preserved in salt and sugar and used in the Hakka speciality *mui choy kau yoke*, pork belly with preserved mustard greens.

Noodles
Chinese noodles are made mainly from wheat flour or rice flour, although some are made using mung bean flour, sweet potato flour or buckwheat flour. Generally, wheat noodles (*mian tiao, meen*) are eaten in northern China, while rice noodles are more common in the south. Wheat noodles made with duck eggs and kneaded with a bamboo pole are a Hong Kong speciality. If you're using dried noodles, soak them in warm water first to soften them.

Rice noodles (*mi fen, mai fun*), made with rice flour and water, come in a variety of shapes – some are fine, like hair; others are flat, like fettuccine.

Another variety comes in sheets; these are often sold fresh and can be found in the refrigerated section of Asian grocers. To cook them, the sheets are cut into strips and fried or tossed into soups.

Bean thread noodles, also known as cellophane or glass or mung bean noodles, are made with mung bean starch, not sweet potato flour. They are sold in bundles and become translucent when cooked. They're slippery and tasteless on their own, but they readily absorb the flavours of whatever they are cooked with. A rich source of B vitamins and minerals, they're often used in vegetarian dishes.

Oyster sauce (*hau you, ho yau*)
A Cantonese invention, oyster sauce is made with oyster extract, sugar, soy and flour. It's used as a condiment and in all sorts of dishes.

Rock sugar (*bing tang, bing tong*)
More subtle than refined sugar, rock sugar has a slight caramel flavour and adds a rich lustre to dishes. It's used widely in Shanghainese cuisine.

Sesame oil (*ma you, ma yau*)
Aromatic and strong-flavoured, Chinese sesame oil is made from roasted white sesame seeds. It's used in marinades and added sparingly to dishes towards the end of cooking as a nuanced seasoning. It keeps indefinitely in the refrigerator.

Sesame paste
(*zhi ma jiang, ji ma jeong*)
Chinese sesame paste is made from roasted sesame seeds, and is quite different to the Middle East's tahini. Thick and nutty brown, it's used mostly in Sichuan and northern Chinese cooking. Sold in jars, it has a layer of oil on top; mix to a pouring consistency before using.

Sichuan pepper (*hua jiao, fa jiu*)
Indispensable in Sichuan cookery and a popular seasoning in all Chinese regional styles, Sichuan peppercorns are the tiny berries of a type of prickly ash tree. They're aromatic, with a woody-lemony fragrance, and leave a numbing, tingly sensation on the tongue and lips. Look for peppercorns with a bright colour and strong fragrance. Two kinds are used in Chinese cooking: the reddish-brown type is more popular and readily available than its green cousin. At a pinch, they're interchangeable.

Soy sauce (*jiang you, jeong yau*)
Of all the Chinese ingredients, soy sauce is the most important. Cantonese kitchens use two types: light and dark. Light soy sauce is thinner and more salty. It's made from the first extraction after fermentation and used for cooking and as a dip. Dark soy sauce, made from the second extraction after the light sauce is made, is thicker and stronger. It's used for braising or when a richer colour is needed in a dish. Most commercial soy sauces contain chemicals to hasten fermentation. I recommend using organic brands – the Kowloon Soy Co soy sauce factory in Hong Kong uses the traditional method. Tamari and shoyu are good substitutes.

Tangerine peel, dried
(*chen pi, chan pei*)
Also known as mandarin peel, these pieces of dried peel are prized for their fragrance. They're sold at Asian supermarkets or you can make your own.

Wonton wrappers
(*hun un pi, wan ton pai*)
It's possible to make your own wrappers (also known as wonton skins), but most Chinese cooks would buy them. They can be found in the refrigerated section of Asian supermarkets.

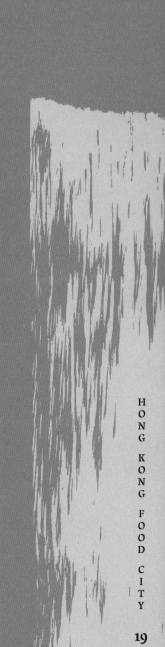

starters, soups and cold dishes

I STILL REMEMBER A LUNCH I WAS INVITED TO YEARS AGO, LONG BEFORE MY FAMILY MOVED TO HONG KONG. IT WAS A STIFLING HOT SUMMER'S DAY AND EVERYONE WAS FEELING LETHARGIC AND NOT TERRIBLY HUNGRY.

But when we tasted the refreshing salad of smashed cucumber flecked with pickled chillies, a tender chilled chicken topped with a vinaigrette made with roasted sesame seed paste, and a divine presentation of century eggs with house-made pickled ginger, our jaded appetites immediately awakened.

Welcome to the fascinating world of Chinese appetisers with its infinite variety of dishes. While we don't generally encounter appetisers or starters – other than dim sum dishes – in most Chinese restaurants in the West, these little dishes are common in Hong Kong. In Cantonese they are called *hoi wai choy* (meaning 'to tease the appetite') or *siu sek* ('little dishes'), and they set the tone for the meal. Often enjoyed when entertaining at home, or on formal occasions such as weddings, they could be compared to the exquisite Mediterranean mezze.

These palate teasers can be modest or elaborate. Some are simple – nothing more than peanuts simmered in soy sauce, silken bean curd with diced crunchy cucumber and a splash of sesame oil and soy, or pickled cabbage with chilli. An elaborate starter could be a pig's ear terrine that requires several hours to make, or crunchy jellyfish paired with boozy abalone – a dish reserved for a fancy dinner party. And, should there be a special occasion, Chinese cooks will offer eight delicacies arranged auspiciously – eight being the lucky number – on an exquisite platter for all to admire. Whatever the

occasion, cold starters are wonderful because they can be made in advance, leaving the cook with time to entertain.

Hong Kong is a fabulous mix of people who've come from all over China and, as such, the different cooking styles have fostered an enormous choice of appetisers seldom seen in the world's Chinatowns or even on mainland China. It's not uncommon to find delicious morsels such as Sichuan sliced pork with a robust chilli sauce served alongside a scrumptious Hokkien (Fujian) seaweed salad. Also, chefs in Hong Kong are an innovative lot. Never afraid to experiment and improvise with techniques and ingredients, they have created new starters such as the addictive sang choy bao – quail wrapped in lettuce leaves – or reinterpreted the ever-popular prawn toast and served it with Worcestershire sauce and sometimes mayonnaise.

In my years of cooking and teaching, I've learnt a few things about Chinese starters. As with all great world cuisines, Chinese dishes reflect the seasons and should be made with top-quality ingredients. They should not only be visually beautiful but the flavour profiles of dishes served for the starter course should cover the range of hot, sour, salty and sweet. Then there's the recurring theme of texture – what is soft must be contrasted with something firm or crunchy, as in the case of sang choy bao.

Another lesson I've learned is never to become stressed when I'm time poor in Hong Kong. If I'm entertaining at the last minute I'll buy a divine roast goose with crisp skin and succulent meat from Michelin-starred Yat Lok and serve it with some pickles. Yat Lok, incidentally, is a no-frills eatery with non-existent service, but I can vouch for its peerless roast goose.

Although hot starters such as the ubiquitous spring roll and fried wontons are popular, chefs and cooks in Hong Kong are adept at turning both unusual and everyday ingredients into the finest mouth-watering appetisers. While some of us will readily discard goose web, for instance, in Hong Kong it's braised for hours with superior stock and tangerine peel until tender. Sea cucumber, on the other hand, is a highly prized delicacy and served as a starter.

Soups are a typical way to start a meal in southern China, while in the north they're eaten towards the end of the meal. Generally served alongside other dishes, soups are indispensable in Chinese food culture. In fact, Cantonese mothers would often tell their daughters that the way to a man's heart was through a good pot of soup.

Traditionally, Chinese soups fall into two categories. The first is the silky, creamy soup that is often thickened with cornflour or potato starch. This style of soup is called 'kang' in Cantonese, and the sweetcorn soup served in Chinese restaurants around the world falls into this category. But, unlike the gloopy versions often seen in the West, properly made soups of this school are lavish and complex. A fine

example is the ever-popular, classic Sichuan hot and sour soup. The second category is that of the renowned clear 'slow fire' soups. These consommé-style preparations are usually made with chicken or pork, goji berries and herbs such as Solomon's seal, and are left to simmer gently in the pot for hours. Although it's made in next to no time for expediency, the winter melon soup in this chapter is in this category.

I've only touched on the tip of the culinary iceberg of Chinese appetisers and soups, but they're important because they help break the ice when guests enter your space – be that at the dining table or in the kitchen. For me, they also create a delicious sense of anticipation.

The recipes in this chapter are wonderfully achievable, and light and refreshing, paving the way to the main course. Start off by making a couple of appetisers and, once you've got the hang of it, increase your repertoire to four, then six and then eight. And voila! You've created the lucky eight, the much-loved number of Chinese people.

Hot and sour soup

I simply adore this soup. Rich and deeply complex, it will bring you much kudos, particularly from guests who love peppery and pungent flavours. There's much debate about its provenance, although most experts believe it's from Sichuan province. Several versions exist, some including chicken's or duck's blood and Sichuan mustard pickle. The heat of the soup relies on pepper rather than chilli, which suggests to me that it predates the arrival of chillies to China.

5 dried shiitake mushrooms
2 tablespoons cloud ear fungi
 (see Note)
30 g (1 oz) dried lily buds (see Note)
150 g (5½ oz) lean pork or chicken,
 sliced into thin strips
1 tablespoon vegetable oil
1 garlic clove, finely chopped
20 g (¾ oz) ginger, finely chopped
2 litres (70 fl oz/8 cups) chicken or
 superior stock (page 241)
200 g (7 oz) soft tofu, cut into
 thin strips
4–5 tablespoons Chinkiang vinegar,
 or to taste

1 tablespoon light soy sauce
2 teaspoons dark soy sauce
2 teaspoons sesame oil
2 teaspoons white pepper, or to taste
2 tablespoons cornflour (cornstarch),
 mixed with 3 tablespoons water
2 eggs, lightly beaten
1 spring onion (scallion),
 thinly sliced

MARINADE
1 teaspoon dark soy sauce
1 teaspoon Shaoxing rice wine
1½ teaspoons cornflour (cornstarch)
 mixed with 1 tablespoon water

Soak the shiitake, cloud ears and lily buds in separate bowls of hot water for 30 minutes. Drain the shiitake mushrooms, trim off and discard the stalks and cut the caps into thin strips. Drain the cloud ears and cut into thin strips. Drain the lily buds and cut off the hard tips, then slice into bite-sized strips. Combine the marinade ingredients, a pinch of salt and 3–4 grinds black pepper in a bowl, add the meat, mix well and leave to marinate for 20 minutes.

Heat the oil in a large saucepan, add the garlic and ginger and fry until fragrant. Add the shiitake mushrooms, cloud ears, lily buds and the stock. Bring to the boil and add the meat, separating it with a fork, then add the tofu, vinegar, soy sauces, sesame oil, white pepper and salt to taste. As soon as the soup returns to the boil, gently stir in the cornflour mixture. Simmer for a minute, then stream in the beaten eggs to form fine threads. Reduce the heat and let the eggs set for 30 seconds. Pour the soup into serving bowls, sprinkle with spring onions and serve.

Note *Cloud ear fungi are available from select Chinese grocers and delicatessens; they're usually sold dried and require soaking in hot water to rehydrate them before use. Lily buds are the dried unopened flowers of daylilies; the Chinese call these 'golden needles' and they are sold in plastic packets at Asian grocers.*

Quail sang choy bao

One of the most recognisable Cantonese dishes, sang choy bao is wonderfully delicious and doesn't require much explanation. Eaten with your hands, these parcels are believed to have originated somewhere in the New Territories, where squab and quail are plentiful. To make the dish really shine, stir-fry the ingredients quickly in a very hot wok for that distinctive *wok hei*, the elusive wok fragrance that distinguishes Cantonese cooking.

12 iceberg lettuce leaves
250 g (9 oz) quail meat, finely diced
3–4 dried shiitake mushrooms,
    soaked in hot water until soft
4–5 water chestnuts, finely chopped
3 tablespoons vegetable oil
1 spring onion (scallion), white part
    only, finely chopped
2 cloves garlic, crushed
3 cm (1¼ inch) piece ginger,
    finely chopped
1 lap cheong sausage, finely diced
50 g (1¾ oz) bamboo shoots, finely
    chopped

1 tablespoon oyster sauce
3 tablespoons chicken stock
1 teaspoon cornflour (cornstarch),
    mixed with 1 tablespoon water

MARINADE
2 teaspoons light soy sauce
1 tablespoon Shaoxing rice wine
Pinch of Chinese five-spice
½ teaspoon sugar
½ teaspoon cornflour (cornstarch)

Carefully trim the lettuce leaves to form small cups, then soak in iced water briefly to crisp up. Drain and refrigerate.

Combine the marinade ingredients in a bowl, add the quail and mix well, then set aside for 20 minutes. Meanwhile, drain the shiitake mushrooms, slice off the stems and squeeze excess water from the caps. Dice the mushrooms so they're a similar size to the diced water chestnuts.

Heat 1 tablespoon oil in a wok over medium–high heat and stir-fry the quail and spring onion until just starting to brown. Remove from the wok and keep warm. Wipe out the wok with paper towel and add the remaining oil. When hot, add the garlic and ginger, stir-fry for 30 seconds, then add the mushrooms, water chestnuts, lap cheong and bamboo shoots. Continue to stir-fry for 30 seconds.

Add the oyster sauce and chicken stock. Return the quail and spring onion to the wok, stir-fry for a further minute, season to taste with salt and white pepper, then add the cornflour mixture and blend well. Serve on a warmed plate with the lettuce leaves to wrap the quail filling into parcels.

STARTERS SOUPS AND COLD DISHES

Sichuan sliced pork with garlic and chilli sauce

This popular cold starter, also known as white-cut pork, is perfect for summer entertaining or any family meal. It involves a technique that's used throughout China, but the dish doesn't appear on restaurant menus because it's considered too plebeian. Traditionally, the meat is poached in water (although some cooks use chicken stock) until it's just cooked, then sliced and served with a dipping sauce. I've used thick-end belly pork here, but chicken and lamb work equally well. This is best made a day in advance to allow the meat to firm up before it's cut into thin slices. Here I serve it with a Sichuan dipping sauce, although by all means experiment and perhaps serve it with pickled Chinese cabbage (page 245) or Shanghai-style cloud ear fungus salad (page 34).

500 g (1 lb 2 oz) lean pork belly, skin on
2 tablespoons Shaoxing rice wine
10 g (¼ oz) piece ginger, crushed
2 tablespoons chopped spring onion (scallion)
    or coriander (cilantro)

GARLIC AND CHILLI SAUCE
1 tablespoon finely chopped garlic
1 spring onion (scallion), finely chopped
1 long red or green chilli
2 tablespoons Sichuan dark soy sauce (see Note)
    or regular dark soy sauce
1 tablespoon clear rice vinegar, or to taste
¼ teaspoon ground Sichuan peppercorn
2 teaspoons chilli oil, or to taste

Put the pork in a large saucepan and cover with cold water. Bring to the boil, reduce the heat and simmer for 5 minutes, then discard the water and rinse the pork and saucepan. Return the pork to the pan, add the Shaoxing rice wine and ginger, season with salt, cover with cold water and bring to the boil. Reduce the heat to a bare simmer and cook for 20–30 minutes or until the pork is just cooked. To test, insert a knife into the thickest part; if the juices run clear, it's cooked. Turn off the heat and leave the pork to steep for 15 minutes.

Remove the pork from the poaching liquid (reserve for another use), cool completely, then cover with plastic wrap and refrigerate overnight to firm up.

To make the garlic and chilli sauce, mix all the ingredients in a bowl.

To serve, slice the rind off the pork, then slice the pork across the grain into paper-thin slices, arrange on a serving plate, pour a little sauce over the top and scatter with spring onion, coriander or greens of your choice.

Note

Sichuan dark soy sauce is made with 500 ml (17 fl oz/2 cups) soy sauce, 100 g (3½ oz) brown or rock sugar, 1 star anise, 1 small piece cinnamon bark, 1 piece liquorice and 1 black cardamom pod. Bring all the ingredients to the boil and simmer until reduced by a third. Leave to cool, then strain. Store in the refrigerator.

Bang bang chicken

Serves 4-6

Also known as 'strange-flavour chicken', bang bang chicken gets its name from the sound of a mallet pounding a piece of chicken on a chopping board. A popular dish from Sichuan, it's essentially poached chicken dressed with a nutty, hot and numbing sauce.

1 litre (35 fl oz/4 cups) chicken stock
1 tablespoon Shaoxing rice wine
500 g (1 lb 2 oz) skinless chicken breast fillets
    or boned chicken Marylands (leg quarters)
1 tablespoon roasted sesame seeds or peanuts
1 small red chilli, thinly sliced (optional)

DRESSING
3 tablespoons Chinese roasted sesame paste
    (see Note)
2 tablespoons light soy sauce
1 tablespoon Chinkiang vinegar
2 teaspoons sugar, or to taste
2 teaspoons sesame oil
1 tablespoon chilli oil
½ teaspoon chilli flakes
1 teaspoon crushed Sichuan peppercorns
2 tablespoons chicken stock

SALAD
2 spring onions (scallions), thinly sliced
1 handful of coriander (cilantro) sprigs
1 small cucumber, cut into short batons

Put the stock and Shaoxing rice wine in a saucepan and bring to the boil. Rub the chicken with salt and poach in the simmering stock for 15–20 minutes or until just cooked. Remove the chicken from the stock (reserve for another use) and leave to cool.

Meanwhile, whisk the dressing ingredients in a small bowl and season to taste with salt.

Beat the chicken lightly with a rolling pin or mallet to loosen the fibres. Using your fingers, shred the chicken into long strips along the grain. Transfer to a serving plate, add the salad ingredients and toss to combine. Drizzle with dressing to taste and sprinkle with sesame seeds or peanuts and sliced chilli, if using. Serve with extra dressing on the side.

Note *Chinese roasted sesame paste is available from select Asian grocers. If you don't have any, use tahini.*

STARTERS SOUPS AND COLD DISHES

32

Shanghai-style cloud ear fungus salad with coriander

Serves 2-4

Also known as black fungus, cloud ear fungus is valued by the Chinese for its texture and medicinal properties. Although it's possible to find these exotic mushrooms fresh in the refrigerated sections of select Chinese grocers and delicatessens, they're usually sold dried and require soaking in hot water to rehydrate them. These soft, crunchy and flavourless yet versatile mushrooms are very popular in salads and braised dishes. This simple refreshing salad is easy to make and highlights the beauty of this lesser-known ingredient.

½ cup (10 g/¼ oz) dried cloud ear fungi
3 tablespoons chopped coriander (cilantro)

DRESSING
2 small garlic cloves, finely chopped
1 long red chilli, seeded and chopped,
   or to taste
1 tablespoon Chinkiang vinegar
1 tablespoon light soy sauce
½ teaspoon sesame oil
1 tablespoon vegetable oil
½ teaspoon sugar

Soak the fungus in hot water for 30 minutes to rehydrate. Trim off and discard any knobbly bits, and tear the larger mushrooms into bite-sized pieces.

Bring a saucepan of water to the boil and tip in the fungus. Simmer for 2–3 minutes until softened, then tip into a colander. Rinse under cold running water and drain well.

To make the dressing, whisk the ingredients together in a bowl.

To serve, arrange the fungus and coriander in a bowl, drizzle with dressing and toss to combine.

Drunken abalone

If you come across the term 'drunken' in Chinese cookbooks, it means an ingredient – usually poultry or seafood – has been steeped in Shaoxing rice wine. The cooking technique is said to be as ancient as the city of Shaoxing, where the famed sherry-like rice wine originated. Drunken dishes are not only a joy to eat, they're easy to make, and are always served at room temperature as appetisers. One of the best places to try drunken dishes is Zhejiang Heen in Wan Chai. Run like a club by the Zhejiang Fraternity Association, this restaurant serves superb classics from China's eastern region. Abalone works beautifully in a drunken dish. In this recipe chef and restaurant consultant Daniel Cheung has given a fresh twist to the dish by using Japanese dashi. It's stunning. Daniel suggests finishing it with one or more of the garnishes below.

1 piece kombu
1 teaspoon dashi powder
8 x 70 g (2½ oz) baby abalone (see Note),
    preferably live
400 ml (14 fl oz) Shaoxing rice wine
10 g (¼ oz) slice ginger
1 teaspoon sugar, or to taste
½ teaspoon sea salt, or to taste
1 tablespoon goji berries (optional)

GARNISHES
Dried shrimp roe
Bottarga (salted and dried fish roe), sliced
    on a Microplane
Coriander (cilantro) leaves
Julienned chillies
Finely chopped chives
Salmon roe

Put 500 ml (17 fl oz/2 cups) water and the kombu in a small saucepan, bring to the boil, then turn off the heat and discard the kombu. Stir in the dashi powder to dissolve and leave to cool.

Put the abalone in a steamer on a saucepan of simmering water over medium heat, cover and steam for 4 minutes. Leave to cool, then, using a tablespoon, remove each abalone from its shell, cut off the liver and the frilly skirt and scrub clean. Reserve the shells.

Combine the cool dashi stock, Shaoxing rice wine, ginger, sugar, salt and goji berries in a bowl. Stir until the sugar and salt have dissolved, then add the abalone. Chill in the fridge in a covered container for at least 8 hours or up to 2 days. Bring to room temperature before serving.

To serve, slice the abalone and divide among the shells. Spoon on some of the sauce and top with your choice of garnish.

Note

If fresh abalone isn't available, frozen abalone is sold in select fish shops and Asian supermarkets.

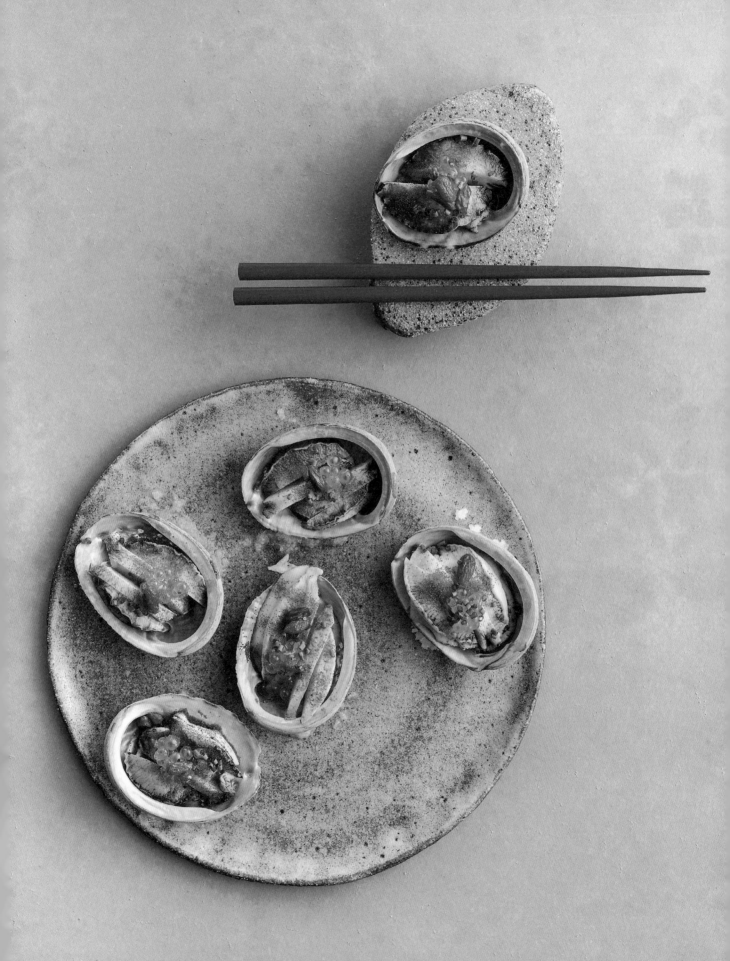

Prawn toast

Serves 8

I don't remember precisely when I first ate this delicious finger food – probably at one of the glamorous dim sum restaurants along Kowloon's Nathan Road. I'm curious about where it originated; after all, Western-style bread was introduced to Hong Kong when the British arrived. Prawn toast is pretty easy to make and I serve it with soy sauce, Worcestershire sauce and sometimes chilli sauce.

350 g (12 oz) uncooked prawn meat
1 egg white
1 garlic clove
1 teaspoon finely chopped ginger
2 teaspoons light soy sauce
Pinch of sugar
1 tablespoon cornflour (cornstarch)
½ teaspoon sesame oil
1 spring onion (scallion), finely chopped
8 slices white bread, crusts removed
Sesame seeds, to serve
Vegetable oil, for shallow-frying

Put all the ingredients except the spring onion, bread, sesame seeds and oil in a food processor, season with salt and white pepper and blend to a smooth paste. Transfer to a bowl and mix in the spring onion. Cover with plastic wrap and refrigerate for 30 minutes to chill.

Spread prawn paste on each slice of bread right to the edges. Put the sesame seeds on a plate. Cut each slice of bread diagonally into triangles and press prawn-side down into the sesame seeds.

Heat 2–3 cm (1 inch) oil in a frying pan to 180°C (350°F) or until a cube of bread dropped in turns golden in seconds. Fry the bread in batches prawn-side down until golden and crisp. Turn and fry for another 30 seconds or until golden. Drain on paper towel and serve hot with a dipping sauce of your choice.

STARTERS SOUPS AND COLD DISHES

38

Winter melon soup with chicken velvet

Often served at Cantonese banquets, winter melon soup is an expression of finesse and purity. The whole melon – weighing some 4–5 kilograms – is usually carved decoratively and used as the serving vessel. It's then steamed with superior stock and luxurious items such as dried scallops and Yunnan ham in a giant steamer. However, this is not practical and I've adapted the recipe to suit the domestic kitchen.

A member of the gourd family, winter melon, despite its name, is available year round. 'Winter' refers to the white coating on the skin, which resembles frost. Like zucchini or marrow, the melon has no distinct flavour but absorbs those it's cooked with. This soup uses a Chinese technique known as 'velveting' – the chicken is mixed with egg white and cornflour before it's cooked so the meat remains soft and tender on the palate.

400 g (14 oz) skinless chicken breast, cut into
    1 cm (½ inch) cubes
2.5 litres (87 fl oz/10 cups) chicken stock
2 teaspoons dried shrimp, rinsed (optional)
500 g (1 lb 2 oz) peeled, seeded winter melon,
    cut into 2 cm (¾ inch) cubes
1 tablespoon Shaoxing rice wine
1 tablespoon light soy sauce
1 spring onion (scallion), finely chopped

VELVETING INGREDIENTS
1 egg white
1 tablespoon Shaoxing rice wine
1 tablespoon cornflour (cornstarch)

To velvet the chicken, combine the egg white and Shaoxing rice wine in a bowl. Add the cornflour and a pinch of salt and mix well until smooth. Add the chicken and set aside for 20 minutes.

Put the chicken stock and dried shrimp, if using, in a large saucepan and bring to the boil. Reduce the heat and simmer for 4–5 minutes, then add the winter melon and simmer for 3 minutes or until it turns opaque.

Increase the heat and add the diced chicken. Stir in the Shaoxing rice wine and soy sauce and simmer until the chicken is cooked through (2–3 minutes). Season to taste and pour the soup into a large tureen or individual bowls. Sprinkle with spring onions and serve hot.

Spinach soup with salted egg and century egg

Apparently, this light and refreshing soup has only recently been on offer in Chinese restaurants, but it has long been made by Cantonese families. Taking just minutes to prepare, it's traditionally made with green amaranth or young spinach leaves and is a surreptitious way of introducing kids – and adults – to the Chinese delicacy century eggs. If you're unfamiliar with century eggs, they don't require cooking. Sweet goji berries, packed with antioxidants, are frequently used in the soup but not essential.

1 tablespoon vegetable oil
1 garlic clove, finely chopped
2 red Asian shallots, finely chopped
2 thin slices ginger
1.5 litres (52 fl oz/6 cups) chicken stock
1 tablespoon goji berries
200 g (7 oz) baby spinach leaves
2 salted duck eggs (see page 247), boiled, peeled
    and chopped
2 century eggs (see Note), peeled and chopped

Heat the oil in a saucepan over medium heat, add the garlic, shallots and ginger and fry until fragrant.

Add the stock and goji berries, bring to the boil and simmer for 2–3 minutes. Taste the soup and add a little salt and white pepper if necessary. Increase the heat to high, add the spinach and cook until just wilted.

Ladle the hot soup into serving bowls or a tureen. Scatter with the salted and century eggs and serve.

Note *Century eggs are duck or quail eggs preserved in a mixture of rice husks, lime, ash and salt; they're available from Asian supermarkets.*

Seaweed salad with sakura shrimp

Serves 2-4

Coastal Chinese, in particular the Hokkien (also known as Fujian) people, are fond of using seaweed in their cooking. I first had this refreshing salad at Putien, a casual restaurant in Causeway Bay that specialises in Hokkien dishes. Flecked with tiny sakura shrimp, this gorgeous salad is a revelation – it's extremely nutritious and perfect for a summer's day when you don't feel like cooking. In the West sakura shrimp, which takes its name from the Japanese word for cherry blossom, is sold frozen and can be used straight from the bag. If laver, a type of seaweed, isn't available, use wakame (both are available from Asian supermarkets) and substitute any dried shrimp if sakura shrimp isn't available. This recipe is a riff on the salad I had at Putien.

20 g (¾ oz) dried laver
1 tablespoon rice wine vinegar
1 teaspoon light soy sauce
½ teaspoon sesame oil
Pinch of sugar, to taste
1 tablespoon sakura shrimp
1 tablespoon vegetable oil
90 g (3¼ oz) cucumber, diced
1 tablespoon thinly sliced spring onion (scallion)

Put the laver in boiling water for 5–10 seconds, then immediately tip into a colander. Rinse under cold running water, then press gently to drain off the excess water. Place in a serving bowl.

Whisk together the rice wine vinegar, light soy sauce, sesame oil and sugar to make a dressing, then add to the seaweed.

Fry the shrimp in the oil over medium heat for 10 seconds, then toss with the seaweed. Stir in the cucumber and spring onion, check the seasoning and serve chilled.

Smashed cucumber salad

Serves 2-4

In Hong Kong and on the mainland, a plate of refreshing smashed cucumbers is considered the perfect summer dish. A Chinese technique, smashing or bruising a cucumber cracks the skin and releases the seeds, leaving the flesh in gorgeous jagged pieces. The cucumber is salted to draw out the moisture and concentrate the flavour, and a simple dressing creates a salad in minutes. This is a much-loved salad and every Chinese family has variations of the dish. Some add ground Sichuan peppercorns, others add sesame paste. My mother loved to include chopped dried shrimps. Once you've got the smashing technique right, by all means experiment; just don't whack the cucumber to smithereens. A note of caution: like cider vinegar, Chinese rice vinegars vary in sharpness – adjust the quantity to suit your palate.

1 large cucumber or 2 Lebanese cucumbers
    (about 300 g/10½ oz)
1 handful of chopped coriander (cilantro), to garnish

DRESSING
2 teaspoons finely chopped pickled chillies
2 small garlic cloves, finely chopped
3 tablespoons clear rice vinegar, or to taste
Pinch of sugar
1 tablespoon chilli oil, or to taste
1 teaspoon sesame oil

Place the cucumber on a chopping board and whack it gently with a cleaver a few times until it splinters and opens up with jagged edges. Cut it into bite-sized pieces and place in a bowl. Sprinkle with ½ teaspoon salt and set aside for 15–20 minutes. Drain off the liquid and place the cucumber in a bowl.

    To make the dressing, put the chillies, garlic, vinegar, sugar and a pinch of salt in a small bowl. Stir in the chilli oil and sesame oil. Pour the dressing over the cucumber and garnish with coriander.

STARTERS SOUPS AND COLD DISHES

46

meat

LONG BEFORE NOSE-TO-TAIL COOKING BECAME FASHIONABLE, THE CHINESE WERE USING JUST ABOUT EVERY PART OF THE ANIMAL.

This becomes obvious when you visit any of the numerous wet markets in Hong Kong. Here, under the glow of the trademark red lamps, every part of the beast is hung in glorious splendour. Butchers with menacing cleavers slice meat, from whole carcasses to offal, with the precision of surgeons, while simultaneously dispensing cooking tips with the ease of trained chefs.

The meat in question is pork; I have to add that no other race 'does' pork better than the Chinese. Much loved for its sweet flavour, pork is so highly regarded that when the Chinese talk meat, they mean pork. Because of this love affair, Chinese cooks have developed a repertoire of pork cookery that is almost limitless – how it is cooked and which restaurant makes the best *siu mei* (the umbrella term for roast meats) is talked about incessantly on television and on social media.

Char siu (meaning 'fork roast') is the much-loved glossy, salty-sweet Cantonese barbecue pork belonging to this genre. In this food-mad city, consumers readily cross town to queue for hours for this delicacy. Just go to Joy Hing, a restaurant in Wan Chai, and you'll discover what I mean. At this fast-paced, bare-bones, non-English-speaking eatery the char siu glistens. Should you go, ask for *ssam bou fan*, the holy trinity of char siu, soy chicken and roast duck. If you prefer your char siu in more sophisticated surroundings, head for Tin Lung Heen at the Ritz-Carlton. Made with prime Ibérico pork shoulder with an even distribution of fat and lean meat, the barbecued pork is sublime and tender.

The love of pork is so entrenched in Chinese culture that the 11th-century poet Su Dongpo even wrote a verse on this versatile meat. The legendary dish from Hangzhou known as Dongpo pork is said to have been created by him. It's made with pork belly, which the Cantonese call *ng fa yoke*, meaning 'five-flower meat' for its alternate layers of fat and lean meat. Extraordinarily delicious, this dish is made with soy sauce, sugar and Shaoxing rice wine and slow-cooked until the fat in the meat turns jelly-like. The Shanghai red-cooked pork in this chapter is similar to this famed dish.

Unsurprisingly, Chinese cooks in Hong Kong have come up with ingenious ways to use every part of the pig, and adventurous diners are more than happy with this guts-and-all approach. The fat is rendered into lard for stir-frying with lean meat, while the skin is either sun-dried or deep-fried into puffy, crunchy pieces (not dissimilar to the Spanish *chicharrón*) or simmered for hours until it turns gelatinous for making *xiao long bao*, the glorious dumpling from Shanghai. As for the lungs, they're made into tonic soups, and the liver is either stir-fried with seasonal greens or made into old-school dumplings as offered in the rough-and-tumble dim sum institution Lin Heung Teahouse. Collagen-rich trotters are given to birthing mothers; cooked for hours with lots of wok-roasted ginger and sweetened black rice vinegar, it's believed this dish not only helps them lactate but also improves their circulation. If trotters are your thing, it makes for exceptionally good eating.

Pork is used for lap cheong, Cantonese pork sausages speckled with fat and infused with a potent rose-flavoured spirit called Mei Kuei Lu Chiew. It's also used to make lap yuk, cured belly pork flavoured with soy sauce. Both of these are used in claypot rice, a comforting winter dish (see page 178).

While it's undeniable that pork cookery has a unique place in Chinese gastronomy, beef certainly holds its own with the Hong Kong Chinese. Perhaps this has something to do with the city's proximity to Shunde in Guangzhou, from where many of Hong Kong's most brilliant chefs hail, but there's a canon of both traditional and innovative beef dishes. Two of the most famous are beef in oyster sauce, and stir-fried beef with black beans. For both, there's a tendency for Cantonese cooks to tenderise the meat by adding bicarbonate of soda. This is partly due to the poor quality of beef that was historically sold in markets – traditionally, oxen were regarded as beasts of burden. However, tenderising beef is unnecessary in the West since the meat is generally hung.

One of my favourite beef dishes is the ever-popular braised brisket. A rich, nourishing street food, perfumed with star anise, Sichuan peppercorns and ginger, and refreshed with daikon some minutes before serving, this is one of the nostalgic dishes my sister made for me when I was a child. It's a dish that will bring a tear to the eye of many Hongkongers when they long for the comforts of home. If you're a beef brisket lover and not particularly concerned about sharing a table, you

simply must go to Kau Kee, virtually an institution at more than 90 years old.

Another notable staple is beef hor fun (page 168). Sold at many *dai pai dong* street stalls and high-end Cantonese establishments, it's made with strips of beef, fresh rice noodles and bean shoots. Properly cooked, the noodles sing with the sensational elusive wok fragrance and the tender beef is beautifully coated with sauce. Easy to rustle up, this is one dish I cook whenever I feel homesick for Hong Kong.

Apart from in a handful of Uighur and Chinese-Muslim restaurants scattered throughout the city, lamb dishes are not often featured in traditional Cantonese eateries. Perhaps because there's little pasture land in the region. Lamb is also considered 'heating' in traditional Chinese medicine – two popular winter dishes are lamb hotpot and braised lamb with bean curd sticks (page 74).

While most of the recipes that follow in this chapter are essentially Cantonese and Chinese, it pays to remember that Hong Kong is vastly cosmopolitan. Chefs and passionate cooks from all over the world have contributed to its ever-changing foodscape, including the long-established Indian community. So you'll find pukka British fare with HP sauce (which, incidentally, has snuck into the Cantonese food world) along with some of the best curries outside India and Pakistan.

Stewed beef brisket

Serves 4-6

Although it might not be as recognisable as wonton soup and dim sum, Hong Kong's stewed beef brisket is another favourite. It's similar to Vietnam's beef pho, the difference being the mix of spices. There are several versions of this delectable dish, but the most well known include beef cooked with oyster sauce, a Cantonese creation called *chu hou* sauce, and, the most popular, beef braised in a clear broth. Noodles often accompany this divine stew, although at home I tend to enjoy it just with oyster sauce and chilli sauce. Two of the best places to try this stewed beef are Sister Wah in Tin Hau, and Kau Kee in Central. The latter started business from a cart some 90 years ago and a constant queue, which often includes local movie stars who happily share a table, is testament to its legendary status. Just don't expect silver service at this rough-and-tumble joint. This recipe is extremely easy to make but you need patience – it takes time for it to become deliciously unctuous.

1 kg (2 lb 4 oz) beef brisket
400 g (14 oz) daikon, peeled and cut into chunks
20 g (¾ oz) ginger, sliced
2 star anise
4 bay leaves
1 teaspoon Sichuan peppercorns
1 teaspoon white peppercorns
2 pieces dried tangerine peel

1 tablespoon rock sugar or raw sugar
2 tablespoons Shaoxing rice wine (optional)
3 tablespoons vegetable oil
2 garlic cloves, chopped
1 spring onion (scallion), thinly sliced
Oyster sauce and chilli sauce, to serve (optional)

Put the beef in a saucepan and cover with water. Bring to the boil, then reduce to a simmer and cook for 8–10 minutes. Remove with a slotted spoon and rinse under cold water. Cook the daikon in the same water for 2–3 minutes, then remove with a slotted spoon and rinse under cold water. Rinse the saucepan.

Tie the ginger, star anise, bay leaves, Sichuan peppercorns, white peppercorns and tangerine peel in a muslin bag with kitchen string and put it into the saucepan. Or add the ingredients directly to the saucepan. Add the beef and sugar and cover completely with water. Bring to the boil, then reduce the heat to low and simmer, partially covered, for 1½ hours or until the beef is fork tender.

Remove the beef and discard the muslin bag or use a fine-meshed strainer to remove the spices. Add the daikon to the hot stock and cook until tender (12–15 minutes). Add the Shaoxing rice wine and season with salt to taste.

Put the vegetable oil in a small saucepan over medium heat. Add the garlic and stir with wooden chopsticks until light brown. Strain the oil and discard the garlic.

To serve, slice the beef into soup bowls. Ladle the radish and soup over the top, scatter with spring onions and drizzle with garlic oil. Offer oyster sauce and chilli sauce. Serve with rice or noodles.

Note
Rock sugar is available from Asian grocers. It needs to be crushed before using; the best way to do this is to put it in a snaplock bag and whack it with a meat mallet.

Sweet and sour pork

Serves 4

For many Chinese people, especially those from Guangdong province, sweet and sour pork speaks of nostalgia and family meals. Known as *gu lou yuk*, meaning 'pork with a long history', this stand-out traditional dish is nothing like the horrors I've been served in the West.

From humble eateries in the New Territories and hole-in-the-wall kitchens in North Point to glamorous restaurants such as Mott 32 and Duddell's, sweet and sour pork charms diners in its various permutations. Some cooks stick to the tried and tested, as I have in this recipe, while others go for ingredients such as dragon fruit and dried hawthorn mixed with plum juice. Most cooks agree that the dish is one of the benchmarks of Cantonese cooking, although I'm told the original version used pork spare ribs.

A great sweet and sour pork should be light, with a fine balance of sweet and sour flavours, and the pieces of pork should be crunchy on the outside and juicy within. It should be served immediately so that each ingredient remains crisp.

Sweet and sour pork isn't difficult to make, but, as with most Chinese cooking, it requires a bit of planning and time. First, you need to select the cut of pork. For me, pork neck is best because it has a good distribution of lean meat and fat. There are no hard-and-fast rules about the greens to use, but it's important to include garlic, onion and spring onion. Traditionally, most Cantonese cooks incorporate capsicums, sometimes pineapple and young ginger or chillies in the mix. Once you've made this version, I'm sure you'll never go back to a mediocre Chinese restaurant for sweet and sour pork again.

500 g (1 lb 2 oz) pork neck, cut into
    3 cm (1 inch) cubes
vegetable oil, for deep-frying
135 g (4¾ oz/¾ cup) potato flour
125 g (4½ oz/¾ cup) rice flour
1 small brown onion, cut into wedges
2 garlic cloves, finely chopped
2–3 long red chillies, seeded and
    thinly sliced
80 g (2¾ oz/½ cup) chopped red
    capsicum (pepper)
80 g (2¾ oz/½ cup) bite-sized pieces
    fresh pineapple
1 spring onion (scallion), cut into
    5 cm (2 inch) batons
1 firm tomato, cut into wedges

MARINADE
1 scant teaspoon Chinese five-spice
2 teaspoons light soy sauce
2 teaspoons Shaoxing rice wine
1 teaspoon ginger juice (squeezed
    from 2 tablespoons grated ginger)
1 egg, beaten

SWEET AND SOUR SAUCE
125 ml (4 fl oz/½ cup) tomato sauce
    (ketchup), mixed with 185 ml
    (6 fl oz/¾ cup) chicken stock
1 tablespoon sugar, or to taste
1 tablespoon white rice vinegar,
    or to taste
2 teaspoons light soy sauce
½ teaspoon dark soy sauce
½ teaspoon sesame oil
1 teaspoon potato flour, mixed with
    1 tablespoon water

Continued overleaf

Combine the marinade ingredients and a pinch of salt in a bowl. Add the pork and mix well to coat. Cover with plastic wrap and refrigerate for 20 minutes.

For the sweet and sour sauce, combine the ingredients except the potato flour mixture in a bowl, season to taste with salt and pepper, and adjust the sugar and vinegar to taste. Set aside.

Heat oil for deep-frying in a wok to 185°C (365°F) or until a piece of bread browns in 10 seconds. Combine the potato flour and rice flour in a bowl. Add the pork and toss to coat evenly, then deep-fry in batches for 3-4 minutes until golden brown and crisp (take care: hot oil will spit). Remove the pork with a slotted spoon and drain on paper towel. Repeat for an even crisper texture.

Strain the oil into a heatproof container and reserve for another use. Wipe out the wok with paper towel, return to the heat and add 1 tablespoon of the reserved oil. When hot, add the onion, garlic and chillies and stir-fry for 30 seconds. Add the capsicum and pineapple and stir-fry for another 20 seconds, then add the sweet and sour sauce and bring to the boil.

Stir in the potato flour mixture and stir until thickened. Check the seasoning and add the spring onion, tomato and pork. Warm through and serve with steamed rice.

Korean spicy pork wraps

Hong Kong is famous for its private kitchens, where talented, cash-strapped chefs set up shop in their apartments or in obscure industrial sites to showcase their cooking. Offering anything from traditional Chinese to modern creations from around the globe, private kitchens have been part of the dining scene in Hong Kong since the 1990s. I met Korean-American Mina Park a couple of years ago when she hosted a dinner at her apartment and was impressed by her passion for cooking. A high-flying former corporate lawyer, Mina produces Korean-inspired dining events under the name Sook. This is her recipe, and she suggests eating this delicious grilled pork wrapped in lettuce leaves.

1 kg (2 lb 4 oz) pork belly or neck,
    sliced 5 mm (¼ inch) thick
Vegetable oil, for frying

MARINADE
20 g (¾ oz) ginger, finely chopped
25 g (1 oz) garlic, crushed
½ brown onion, finely chopped
2 teaspoons sesame oil
3 tablespoons light soy sauce
3 tablespoons mirin
2 spring onions (scallions), finely
    chopped
50 g (1¾ oz) gochugaru (Korean
    chilli powder; see Note)

SSÄMJANG SAUCE
40 g (1½ oz) doenjang
    (soy bean paste; see Note)
40 g (1½ oz) gochujang
    (red chilli paste; see Note)
10 g (¼ oz) honey
1 tablespoon mirin
1 teaspoon grated ginger
1 teaspoon grated garlic
1 tablespoon roasted sesame seeds

TO SERVE
Chopped spring onions (scallions)
Coriander (cilantro)
Chopped avocado
Kimchi
Lettuce leaves
Steamed rice

Combine all the marinade ingredients in a large bowl and add the pork. Cover with plastic wrap and refrigerate for at least 4 hours or preferably overnight.

For the ssämjang sauce, combine the ingredients in a bowl.

Brush a chargrill pan with oil and set it over high heat. Cook the pork in batches in a single layer for 4–5 minutes each side (depending on the thickness of the slices) until nicely browned and just cooked through.

Cut the pork into bite-sized pieces and serve with spring onions, coriander, avocado, kimchi, lettuce leaves, steamed rice and ssämjang sauce.

Note *Gochugaru, doenjang and gochujang are available at Asian grocers.*

2-HOUR METER
Operating he
monday to sa
sunday & pu
In case of me
The meter humber me

二小時停車
收費時間:
星期一至星期六由.
星期日及公眾假期
如錶失靈請
並需說明

Char siu (barbecue pork)

Char siu with its sweet and savoury notes has a certain deliciousness that's forever locked in my food memories – it makes my mouth water from the moment I see the honey dripping down the smoky pork in Cantonese *siu mei* restaurants. In Hong Kong this barbecued pork is taken so seriously that food critics debate which establishment makes the best. Some say family-run Joy Hing's in Wan Chai, while others consider Mott 32 with its top-drawer Ibérico de bellota pork the best.

This is a simple recipe. The secret lies in the marinade and basting the pork while it's roasting. This recipe is based on the glorious char siu I've had at One Harbour Road, the Cantonese restaurant at the Grand Hyatt in Wan Chai.

500 g (1 lb 2 oz) shoulder pork
2 garlic cloves, finely chopped
Thinly sliced spring onions (scallions), to serve

MARINADE
1 tablespoon light soy sauce
1 teaspoon dark soy sauce
½ teaspoon white pepper
1 tablespoon hoisin sauce
2 cubes red fermented bean curd, mashed
½ teaspoon Chinese five-spice
1 tablespoon honey
1 tablespoon Mei Kuei Lu Chiew liquor (see Note)
A few drops red food colouring (optional)

Cut the pork lengthways into strips 5 cm (2 inches) wide and 2.5 cm (1 inch) thick and put into a non-reactive container. Combine the marinade ingredients in a saucepan over low heat and stir together. Leave to cool, then stir in the garlic and massage the marinade into the pork. Cover with plastic wrap and marinate in the refrigerator for 5–6 hours or overnight.

Preheat the oven to 220°C (425°F). Bring the pork back to room temperature and drain off the excess marinade into a small bowl. Place the pork on a rack in the middle of the oven and put a roasting pan containing a cupful of hot water underneath on the bottom rack. Roast the meat for 20 minutes, basting with the marinade occasionally. Reduce the oven to 180°C (350°F) and roast for a further 15 minutes or until the internal temperature of the meat reaches 74°C (165°F).

Cool the pork briefly, then cut it into bite-sized pieces. Garnish with spring onions and serve as an appetiser or with steamed rice as a light meal.

Note *Mei Kuei Lu Chiew liquor, which translates as rose dew wine or rose essence, is made with sorghum and rose petals. If it's unavailable, use Shaoxing rice wine.*

M
E
A
T

62

Wagyu short rib, jalapeño purée, soy glaze and spring onion kimchi

Chef Jowett Yu's basement restaurant, Ho Lee Fook, has been a mecca for food lovers since it opened in late 2015. Formerly of Sydney's Ms G and Mr Wong, Taiwan-born Yu is incredibly talented, and his take on modern Chinese food is inspiring. The punters flock to the restaurant for his sensational signature dish of wagyu beef rib with jalapeño purée.

1 x 1.2 kg (2 lb 12 oz) wagyu
    short rib
1 tablespoon light soy sauce
1 tablespoon Shaoxing rice wine
Vegetable oil, for deep-frying
100 g (3½ oz) spring onions
    (scallions), julienned

JALAPEÑO PURÉE
100 g (3½ oz) jalapeño chillies or
    any green chillies
1 brown onion, cut into thick rings
30 g (1 oz) garlic
2½ tablespoons olive oil
25 ml (¾ fl oz) fish sauce

SOY GLAZE
100 ml (3½ fl oz) Japanese light
    soy sauce
100 g (3½ oz) brown sugar
1 teaspoon cornflour (cornstarch),
    mixed with 2 tablespoons water

KIMCHI PASTE
25 ml (¾ fl oz) fish sauce
25 g (1 oz) sugar
25 ml (¾ fl oz) sesame oil
1 tablespoon rice vinegar
1 teaspoon chilli oil
¼ brown onion, chopped
30 g (1 oz) garlic, chopped
1 long red chilli, chopped and seeded
25 g (1 oz) gochugaru (Korean chilli
    powder; see Note)

Preheat the oven to 150°C (300°F), put the beef rib, soy sauce, Shaoxing rice wine and 500 ml (17 fl oz/2 cups) water in a roasting tin, cover tightly with foil and roast for 8–10 hours. Remove the rib (discard the roasting juices) and pat dry with kitchen towel.

For the jalapeño purée, heat a grill and roast the jalapeños until blackened. Grill the onion slowly until caramelised and soft. Grill the garlic until soft, being careful not to let it burn. Transfer all three to a blender, add the olive oil and fish sauce and process until smooth.

For the soy glaze, bring the soy sauce and brown sugar to the boil in a saucepan, stirring until the sugar has dissolved. Add the cornflour mixture and stir until the sauce just coats the back of the spoon.

For the kimchi paste, put everything except the gochugaru in a blender and process until smooth, then add the gochugaru and pulse to combine.

Heat oil in a deep-fryer or large heavy-based saucepan to 170°C (325°F) and deep-fry the short rib for 8 minutes, then slice and dress with a little soy glaze. Toss the julienned spring onions with 1–2 tablespoons of kimchi paste, mix well and serve with the beef rib and jalapeño purée.

Note
Gochugaru is available from Asian grocers.

Hakka pork with preserved mustard greens

Serves 6-8

This is one of the most soulful and rich dishes from the Hakka people, although it's made with humble ingredients. It can be made a day in advance, which makes it perfect for entertaining and also allows the flavours to meld.

You'll need to shop at an Asian grocer for preserved mustard greens. Sold dried in packets and called *muy choy* in Cantonese and *mei cai* in Mandarin, this umami-packed green has a unique and incredible flavour profile. It has several applications in both traditional and modern Chinese cooking. Look out for the versions produced in Zhejiang province or the Stone Crane brand.

For the best results, ask your butcher for lean belly pork.

700 g (1 lb 9 oz) belly pork, skin on
125 ml (4 fl oz/½ cup) vegetable oil
1 tablespoon rock sugar (see Note), finely crushed
2 teaspoons cornflour (cornstarch), mixed with 2 tablespoons water
Spring onions (scallions), to serve

MARINADE
2 tablespoons light soy
2 tablespoons Shaoxing rice wine
½ teaspoon Chinese five-spice

PRESERVED MUSTARD GREENS
180 g (6½ oz) preserved mustard greens
3 tablespoons vegetable oil
2 garlic cloves, finely chopped
2 teaspoons rock sugar
1 tablespoon Shaoxing rice wine
Light soy sauce, to taste

For the marinade, mix the ingredients in a bowl, add the pork, turn to coat well and leave to marinate for 30 minutes. Remove the pork, reserving the marinade, and pat dry with paper towel. Heat the oil in a wok over medium heat, add the pork skin-side down and shallow-fry until it begins to blister. Remove the pork and refresh in iced water to stop it cooking further. When the pork is cool enough to handle, cut it crossways into 2 cm (¾ inch) slices. Arrange the slices neatly in a heatproof bowl and brush with some of the remaining marinade.

Meanwhile, for the preserved mustard greens, rinse the mustard greens to wash off excess salt and soak for 20 minutes in a bowl of cold water. Drain, squeeze out the excess moisture and chop very finely. Heat the oil in a wok over medium heat. Add the garlic and fry until just golden, then add the mustard greens. Fry for 1 minute, then add the rock sugar and Shaoxing. Taste – it should be salty enough to season the pork; otherwise add a little soy sauce.

Spread the mustard greens over the pork. Sprinkle with the sugar and the remaining marinade. Put the bowl in a steamer and steam gently for 3 hours until the pork is very tender. Carefully pour the juices into a small saucepan. Invert the bowl of pork onto a large serving plate and keep warm.

Bring the juices to the boil. Add the cornflour mixture and stir until the sauce thickens. Pour the sauce over the pork and vegetables, sprinkle with sliced spring onions and serve.

Note
Rock sugar is available from Asian grocers. It needs to be crushed before using; the best way to do this is to put it in a snaplock bag and whack it with a meat mallet.

Ma po doufu

This classic Sichuan dish was invented by a widow named Chen at a stall in Chengdu. The name translates as 'pock-marked grandmother's bean curd'. It's made with soft-textured bean curd similar to silken tofu along with chilli flakes, fermented black beans and a chilli bean paste called *doubanjiang*.

50 g (1¾ oz) minced (ground) beef
500 g (1 lb 2 oz) soft bean curd, cut into 3 cm (1¼ inch) cubes
3 tablespoons vegetable oil
2 garlic cloves, finely chopped
1–2 tablespoons chilli bean paste (doubanjiang; see Note)
2 teaspoons fermented black beans
2 teaspoons light soy sauce
1 teaspoon sugar
1 tablespoon chilli oil, or to taste
250 ml (9 fl oz/1 cup) chicken stock
1 baby leek, thinly sliced
1 teaspoon roasted ground Sichuan pepper

1 teaspoon chilli flakes (optional)
30 g (1 oz) Sichuan preserved vegetable (see Note), rinsed and finely chopped
1 teaspoon potato flour, mixed with 2 tablespoons cold water
Chopped spring onions (scallions), to serve

MARINADE
½ teaspoon light soy sauce
½ teaspoon Shaoxing rice wine
½ teaspoon salt
½ teaspoon sugar

Combine the marinade ingredients in a bowl, add the beef, mix well and marinate for 5–10 minutes.

Cook the bean curd in a saucepan of simmering water until warmed through. Drain well and set aside.

Heat a wok over high heat, add the oil, then add the beef and stir-fry for 20 seconds. Add the garlic, reduce the heat to medium and stir in the chilli bean paste, fermented black beans, soy sauce, sugar and chilli oil. Stir-fry for another 30 seconds, then pour in the stock, add the bean curd and stir gently so as not to break up the cubes. Bring to the boil, then reduce heat to simmer for 2 minutes.

Add the leek, Sichuan pepper, chilli flakes and Sichuan preserved vegetable. Stir in the potato flour mixture and simmer until the sauce thickens. Transfer to a serving plate, garnish with spring onions and serve with steamed rice.

Note *The best doubanjiang is from Pixian county in Sichuan. It's very salty so use it sparingly. If you can't find this variety, use Lee Kum Kee doubanjiang. Sichuan preserved vegetable, called* zha cai *in Mandarin or* ja choy *in Cantonese, is often sold in cans or plastic bags in Chinese grocers. Made from the stems of a variety of mustard green, it's brined, then pickled with chilli powder. Rinse off the excess chilli and salt before use.*

Shanghai red-cooked pork

Serves 6-8

Called *hong shao rou* in Mandarin, this is a classic dish that bears all the hallmarks of the Eastern School. Glistening from the combination of caramelised sugar and the region's famed soy sauce, this sumptuous pork is similar in flavour to the legendary Dongpo pork. Named for the reddish hue that develops during the long cooking process, this rich dish can feature additions such as tofu knots, boiled eggs, salted fish and reconstituted cuttlefish. Some cooks also like to embellish it with ginger, spring onions and star anise.

I don't remember when I first learnt how to make this magnificent dish – probably during the time I was learning Mandarin – but I was reminded of its beauty when I spent a glorious evening with friends Janice Leung Hayes and Charmaine Mok at Zhejiang Heen in Hong Kong's Wan Chai district. As this is a fairly hearty dish, I recommend serving it with something light such as stir-fried greens. This is a very forgiving dish – if you prefer a sweeter flavour, add more sugar; if you like your food salty, add more soy sauce.

800 g (1 lb 12 oz) lean belly pork, skin on
1 tablespoon vegetable oil
1 tablespoon crushed rock sugar (see Note)
    or caster (superfine) sugar
125 ml (4 fl oz/½ cup) Shaoxing rice wine
2 tablespoons light soy sauce
2 tablespoons dark soy sauce

Cut the pork into 2–3 cm (1 inch) cubes. Bring a saucepan of water to the boil, add the pork and cook for 5 minutes. Drain and rinse the meat under cold running water.

Heat the oil and sugar in a wok over medium heat and stir-fry until the sugar turns amber. Add the pork, reduce the heat to low and continue to stir-fry until the sugar has coated the meat.

Add the Shaoxing, soy sauces and 500 ml (17 fl oz/2 cups) water. Bring to the boil, then reduce to a simmer, cover with a lid and simmer for 50–60 minutes, stirring occasionally to prevent the meat from catching and adding more water if necessary.

When the pork is cooked to your liking, remove the lid, increase the heat and boil rapidly, stirring, to reduce the sauce to a glossy consistency. Transfer to a serving dish and serve with steamed rice and stir-fried greens.

Note *Rock sugar is available from Asian grocers. It needs to be crushed before using; the best way to do this is to put it in a snaplock bag and whack it with a meat mallet.*

Braised pork ribs

Serves 2-4

This gorgeous recipe for braised ribs is from my friend Janice Leung Hayes. One of the most authoritative food writers in Hong Kong, Janice is the senior director of Little Adventures, a company that customises food and culture tours around the city. Her passion for real food led her to found the Tong Chong Street Market, Hong Kong's first local, sustainable, organic food market. Committed to educating the public about food, she's often described as the Stephanie Alexander of Hong Kong. Ask your butcher for meaty ribs and have them chopped into bite-sized portions.

2 tablespoons Chinkiang vinegar
2 tablespoons light soy sauce
1 tablespoon dark soy sauce
1 tablespoon vegetable oil
600 g (1 lb 5 oz) pork ribs
1 tablespoon Shaoxing rice wine
4 tablespoons crushed rock sugar (see Note)

Combine the Chinkiang vinegar with the light and dark soy sauces in a bowl and set aside.

Add the oil to a heated wok or frying pan, then add the ribs and fry until browned. Drizzle the rice wine over the ribs and toss for about 20 seconds or until the wine has evaporated.

Add the vinegar–soy mixture to the ribs. As soon as the liquid starts to bubble, reduce the heat to low, cover the wok with a lid and simmer for 5 minutes. If the liquid is reducing too quickly, add a little water.

When the sauce is reduced by half, add the rock sugar and stir to prevent the ribs sticking until the sauce is reduced to a molasses-like consistency, most of which will coat the ribs. Keep the heat low or the sauce will split.

Just before serving, taste and adjust with vinegar, sugar and soy for balance. Serve with steamed rice and stir-fried greens.

Note *Rock sugar is available from Asian grocers. It needs to be crushed before using; the best way to do this is to put it in a snaplock bag and whack it with a meat mallet.*

MEAT

72

Braised lamb with bean curd and tangerine peel

You might not see this home-style Cantonese dish in high-end restaurants, but if you were to go to one of Hong Kong's boisterous, friendly neighbourhood eateries in winter, chances are it would be on the menu – lamb is considered particularly good for warding off winter's cold. This fabulous, funky, easy-going dish relies on the cheesy-tasting fermented bean curd to make it sing. Traditionally, dried bean sticks are added, but if you don't have any in your pantry, just skip them.

500 g (1 lb 2 oz) lamb shoulder, cut into 3 cm (1¼ inch) cubes
500 ml (17 fl oz/2 cups) vegetable oil
3 sticks dried bean curd
2 garlic cloves, finely chopped
50 g (1¾ oz) ginger, thickly sliced
1–2 cubes fermented red bean curd, mashed
2 tablespoons Shaoxing rice wine
1 teaspoon sugar
1 piece dried tangerine peel, soaked until soft and torn into pieces
150 g (5 oz/1 cup) bamboo shoots, cut into 2 cm (1 inch) cubes
8 water chestnuts

1 tablespoon oyster sauce
750 ml (26 fl oz/3 cups) chicken stock
1 teaspoon cornflour (cornstarch), mixed with 1 tablespoon water
½ teaspoon sesame oil
coriander (cilantro) sprigs, to serve

MARINADE
1 tablespoon Shaoxing rice wine
2 teaspoons ginger juice
½ teaspoon Chinese five-spice
1 teaspoon light soy sauce
½ teaspoon sesame oil

Place the lamb in a bowl, add the marinade ingredients and mix well. Cover with plastic wrap and refrigerate for 1–2 hours.

Heat the oil in a wok to 170°C (325°F). Break the bean curd sticks into pieces and deep-fry them briefly until they puff up, but do not brown. Transfer with a slotted spoon to a bowl. Pour boiling water over them to cover and leave to soften, then squeeze out the excess moisture. Cut into 5 cm (2 inch) pieces.

Pour the oil from the wok into a heatproof container and reserve for another use. Wipe out the wok with paper towel. Return 2 tablespoons of the oil to the heated wok and fry the garlic and ginger until fragrant. Add the fermented bean curd and fry for a few seconds, then add the lamb and stir-fry for about 1 minute. Add the Shaoxing rice wine, sugar, tangerine peel, bamboo shoots, water chestnuts, oyster sauce and reserved bean curd sticks. Stir for 30 seconds, then add the chicken stock.

Transfer the lamb mixture to a saucepan, ensuring the ingredients are covered by the chicken stock; add more stock if necessary. Cover and simmer, stirring occasionally, for 1–1¼ hours or until the lamb is tender.

Once the lamb is tender, simmer to reduce the sauce by half. Check the seasoning. Add the cornflour mixture and stir until thickened, then add the sesame oil. Garnish with coriander sprigs and serve with steamed rice.

Rogan josh

Around 50,000 Indian and Pakistani people have made Hong Kong their home. Some entered the restaurant trade and offered the regional foods of the Indian subcontinent with local sensibilities. Today, you find outstanding Indian fare all over the city. Rogan josh is a Kashmiri delicacy and for me a reminder of the many wonderful meals I've enjoyed with my Indian friends in Hong Kong.

1 kg (2 lb 4 oz) lamb shoulder, cut into 5 cm (2 inch) cubes
1 litre (35 fl oz/4 cups) chicken or lamb stock
2 teaspoons garam masala (see Note)
Coriander (cilantro), to serve

MARINADE
520 g (1 lb 2½ oz/2 cups) plain yoghurt
Pinch of saffron threads, soaked in 1 tablespoon hot water
2.5 cm (1 inch) piece ginger, chopped
5–8 garlic cloves, chopped
1 large sprig coriander (cilantro), chopped

1 teaspoon Kashmiri chilli powder (see Note)
¼ teaspoon asafoetida (see Note)

MASALA
5 tablespoons vegetable oil or ghee
10 cardamom pods, lightly crushed
2 bay leaves
6 cloves
10 whole black peppercorns
2.5 cm (1 inch) cinnamon stick
1 large brown onion, finely chopped
1 tablespoon finely chopped ginger
3 teaspoons ground coriander
2 teaspoons ground cumin
3 teaspoons paprika, mixed with 2 teaspoons Kashmiri chilli powder
½ teaspoon turmeric powder

For the marinade, mix the yoghurt and saffron with its water in a large bowl. Blend the ginger, garlic, coriander, chilli powder, asafoetida and 2 tablespoons water in a food processor to a smooth paste and add to the yoghurt. Add the lamb and mix well. Refrigerate for 4–6 hours to marinate.

For the masala, heat the vegetable oil or ghee in a heavy-based saucepan over medium–high heat. Add the cardamom, bay leaves, cloves, peppercorns and cinnamon and fry until the cloves swell and the bay leaves begin to colour. Add the onion and fry until golden brown. Add the ginger and fry for a further minute. Mix the coriander, cumin, paprika–chilli mixture and turmeric with 2 tablespoons water, add to the pan and stir for another 1–2 minutes until the oil separates from the spices.

Add the lamb in batches and fry until the yoghurt has been absorbed. Return all the meat to the pan and cover with stock or water. Bring to the boil, scraping up all the browned spices from the bottom of the pan. Cover, reduce the heat to low and simmer, stirring every 10 minutes, for 1 hour or until the meat is tender.

Increase the heat and reduce the stock to a thick sauce. If the meat is very tender, transfer it to a bowl while you reduce the sauce, then return it to the pan.

Sprinkle the rogan josh with garam masala and 1 teaspoon freshly ground black pepper. Garnish with coriander and serve with rice or naan bread.

Note

Garam masala means 'hot spice blend'. There are many good commercial blends, but I encourage you to make your own. Blend 1 tablespoon cardamom seeds, 1 teaspoon cloves, 1 teaspoon black peppercorns and a 5 cm (2 inch) stick of cinnamon to a smooth powder in a coffee grinder. Store in an airtight jar in the refrigerator. Kashmiri chilli powder and asafoetida, a powdered gum resin, are available from Indian grocery stores.

poultry

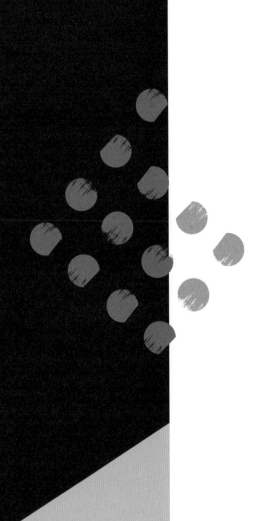

HAVE YOU BEEN TO HONG KONG DURING CHINESE NEW YEAR? IF YOU HAVEN'T, LET ME TELL YOU A STORY...

Chinese New Year is the biggest and most colourful festival in the city, and traditional rituals are observed meticulously. On the days leading up to it, Hong Kong Chinese families spring-clean their homes to bid farewell to any accumulated bad luck, and they flock to flower markets to buy cherry blossoms and pots of jonquils to usher in the New Year. As part of the celebrations, families return home for the all-important New Year's Eve Dinner. Filled with symbolism and traditions, this dinner, also known as the Reunion Dinner, is the most important meal of the year for any Chinese person.

Chicken is of vital importance at this much-anticipated event. On a visit I was told to buy a live chicken. A live chicken? Where was I going to find a free-range bird on the eve of Chinese New Year? And who was going to kill it? What breed of chicken should I buy? Why couldn't we just make do with a frozen bird? The immediate response from the family was: 'We don't eat frozen chicken of dubious quality for Chinese New Year.' The very idea was repugnant to them. But in a city where bird flu has struck, stringent measures have been implemented on the sale of live chickens.

Luckily, a chef told me to head for the chicken vendor in Wan Chai. He dispatched one for me, and I went home with a bird with its head, feet and cleaned giblets intact.

In Chinese culture, a whole chicken symbolises family togetherness and harmony. It also represents the close relationship and unity between married families. Cooked with head and feet attached, it's also used as an offering to the ancestors. As well as the chicken, I cooked six other classic dishes steeped in tradition for the magnificent feast.

Aside from the symbolic significance of chicken in Chinese food culture, it's also much appreciated for its flavour. Until recently, chicken was eaten only on special occasions, so Hongkongers are pretty fastidious about the quality of the birds. My family and many of my Hong Kong friends complain that chickens in Western countries lack flavour. I'm not sure whether this has something to do with the breeds, but generally chickens in Hong Kong taste more delicious.

Take, for instance, the Cantonese poached chicken popularly known as white-cut chicken, served with a dipping sauce of ginger and spring onion. The cooking method is not dissimilar to that of the Hainanese chicken in this chapter, and both require a top-quality bird. That said, Chinese cooks are masters of preparing chicken and the scores of recipes in existence demonstrate their prowess. One of the finest examples is the quintessential Cantonese soy chicken. Steeped in a bath of soy sauces, sugar, star anise and ginger, the bird is wondrously juicy and quite ambrosial.

Although there are many gorgeous chicken dishes using the stir-fry method, such as kung pao chicken, there are others that involve baking, as in the Hakka salt-baked chicken in this chapter. A rustic dish of the once-nomadic Hakka people, this is one dish where the homemade version is far superior to those served in Hong Kong Hakka restaurants; most of them brine and steam the bird, which robs this great dish of its soul.

Man Wah in the Mandarin Oriental Hotel, one of the most elegant and romantic Cantonese restaurants, serves a spectacularly delicious braised chicken with abalone and sand ginger. Sold dried in larger Asian grocers, sand ginger, a rhizome, is a fantastic ingredient with many uses in southern Chinese food.

Meanwhile, duck in the hands of Cantonese and northern Chinese cooks is legendary. Although not regularly cooked at home, duck is adored in Hong Kong, not only as a symbol of fidelity, but also as a source of gastronomic pride. Roast ducks with glossy, lacquered skin are typically seen hanging in the windows of Cantonese restaurants. Properly prepared, Cantonese roast duck has the same crisp crackling skin as Peking duck (page 98), although air isn't pumped into the bird.

Peking duck has a royal pedigree. Legend has it that the dish was smuggled out by the royal cooks during the dying days of the Qing dynasty (1644–1912) and it has spread across the world since. Insanely delicious, this stunning duck is also a visual treat when it's served, expertly sliced by the chef into some 108 pieces. One of the best I've eaten was at Tang Court in the Langham Hotel in Tsim Sha Tsui. I have to add that it's a beauty paired with pinot noir.

Goose is also served mainly in restaurants. Another star of Cantonese *siu mei* or roasting, it's gamey and luscious with a hint of fat. Guide books suggest trying it at Yung Kee in Central,

but if you're prepared to venture to Tai Po out in the New Territories, have the roast goose at Yat Lok Barbecue Restaurant and you'll be a convert. Said to be marinated with 38 spices and herbs, the skin is so crisp that it shatters when you bite into it. This no-frills restaurant has since opened a branch in Central with equally no-nonsense service. For a fresh take on this Cantonese classic, Jowett Yu's version at Ho Lee Fook is superb and certainly up there with the best in town.

Smaller birds such as quail and squab are also very popular in Hong Kong. I recall trekking to the legendary Lung Wah in the New Territories years ago for the dishes of small poultry, but now it's a pale shadow of its glory days. Much better to eat at Kin's Kitchen in Wan Chai for some of the most succulent squab I've had in years. This Cantonese restaurant espouses the farm-to-table ethos and there's even a menu dedicated to all things chicken.

China has seen unimaginable turmoil, caused by man and nature alike, which in turn has affected Hong Kong over the decades. Meat in any form is treated with respect, even if that's not always apparent. Creativity born of necessity is the fulcrum of great cooking, and cooks in this great city have turned the likes of duck tongues, chicken feet and all poultry offal into the most delectable treats.

HONG KONG FOOD CITY

81

Hakka salt-baked chicken

Serves 4-6

A signature dish of the Hakka people, salt-baked chicken frequently appears on restaurant menus in Hong Kong. Traditionally wrapped in salt and baked in a pit until the chicken takes on the distinctive, smoky–salty nuances, this dish is sensational when made properly. Sadly, nowadays most cooks take short cuts and poach or steam a brined chicken, thereby losing the soul of this magnificent dish. It's actually quite an easy recipe, though you might have to seek out sand ginger in an Asian supermarket. If you can't find it, just leave it out – it will be fine. If you visit Hong Kong, try it at Chuen Cheung Kui in Mong Kok.

3 spring onions (scallions), cut into 5 cm
    (2 inch) lengths
1 x 1.8 kg (4 lb) chicken
1 tablespoon ginger juice, squeezed from 50 g (1¾ oz)
    grated ginger
1 tablespoon dark soy sauce
1 tablespoon Shaoxing rice wine
1 teaspoon ground sand ginger
½ teaspoon Chinese five-spice
1 tablespoon vegetable oil
4–5 kg (9–11 lb) coarse salt

GINGER–SPRING ONION SAUCE
100 g (3½ oz) ginger, finely chopped
100 g (3½ oz) spring onions, finely chopped
125 ml (4 fl oz/½ cup) vegetable oil
1 tablespoon oyster sauce

Put the spring onion in the cavity of the chicken. Mix the ginger juice, soy sauce, Shaoxing rice wine, sand ginger, five-spice and ½ teaspoon salt in a small bowl, rub the mixture all over the bird, then refrigerate uncovered for 1–2 hours.

Take the chicken out of the refrigerator an hour before cooking to bring it to room temperature. Rub the oil all over the bird and wrap it neatly in four sheets of baking paper to form a parcel with no gaps. Secure with kitchen string.

Preheat the oven to 180°C (350°F). Line a large roasting tin with foil, add the salt and bake for 20–30 minutes or until very hot. To test the heat, insert a knife into the salt for a few seconds, then remove it – the blade should feel hot to touch.

Transfer half the salt to a large Chinese claypot or casserole, put the chicken on top, breast-side up, and cover with the remaining salt. Cover with a lid and bake at 180°C (350°F) for 1¼ hours or until the juices run clear when the thigh is pierced with a knife.

Meanwhile, to make the sauce, blend the ingredients with a hand-held blender or pound with a mortar and pestle until smooth. Season with salt.

Carefully remove the chicken from the salt. When cool enough to handle, unwrap the chicken and transfer to a chopping board. Cut into portions, arrange on a serving plate and serve with ginger–spring onion sauce.

Kung pao chicken

One of the most famous dishes from Sichuan, kung pao chicken or *gong bao ji ding* is named after a Qing governor of Sichuan, Ding Baozhen, who is believed to have been very partial to it. Hot and spicy, savoury and pungent, versions of this favourite can be found in virtually any Chinese restaurant in Hong Kong. My favourite places to eat this wonderful dish are Yun Yan in Causeway Bay and Sichuan House in Central. Quick and easy to whip up, its success lies in ensuring all the ingredients are cut the same size so they cook evenly. Prawns, calamari, pork, lamb and beef all work well in place of chicken.

350 g (12 oz) skinless chicken thigh
    or breast, cut into 2 cm (¾ inch)
    cubes
8–10 dried long red chillies
2 tablespoons vegetable oil
1 teaspoon Sichuan peppercorns
2 garlic cloves, crushed
2 teaspoons finely chopped ginger
3 spring onions (scallions), white
    part only, cut into short lengths
1 tablespoon Shaoxing rice wine
100 g (3½ oz) roasted peanuts

MARINADE
2 teaspoons light soy sauce
1 teaspoon Shaoxing rice wine
1½ teaspoons cornflour (cornstarch)

SAUCE
3 teaspoons sugar
1 teaspoon light soy sauce
1 teaspoon dark soy sauce
3 teaspoons Chinkiang vinegar
1 teaspoon sesame oil
1 teaspoon cornflour (cornstarch)
2 tablespoons chicken stock

Mix the marinade ingredients, 1 tablespoon water and a pinch of salt in a bowl, add the chicken and set aside for 15–20 minutes.

Snip the chillies into thick sections, discarding as many seeds as possible.

Combine the sauce ingredients and a pinch of salt in a bowl. Taste in case you prefer a stronger flavour – it should taste sweet–sour.

Put 1 tablespoon oil in a wok over medium heat. Add the chillies and Sichuan pepper, lifting the wok away from the heat in case it's too hot – chillies burn easily. Stir-fry until the chillies are crisp and the oil is fragrant.

Quickly add the chicken and stir-fry rapidly until just beginning to turn white, then transfer to a plate. Return the wok to the heat and add the remaining oil. Add the garlic, ginger and spring onions and stir-fry until aromatic. Deglaze the wok with the Shaoxing and return the chicken and chillies to the wok. Stir-fry for 30 seconds or until the meat is cooked through. Stir the sauce and add to the wok. As soon as it thickens, add the peanuts and serve.

Cantonese soy chicken

Serves 4-6

Soy sauce chicken or *see yow gai* is a Cantonese classic. You often see it displayed in the glassed-in section at the front of Chinese restaurants in Chinatowns around the world. It's made by a similar method to Hainanese chicken, except spices are used in the poaching stock. The key to the success of this recipe is to poach the chicken gently so the meat relaxes, ensuring a silky finish. And a good soy sauce makes a great difference to the flavour. Once you've eaten this succulent chicken in all its glory, chances are you'll not buy it ready-made again.

1 x 1.8 kg (4 lb) free-range chicken, fat trimmed

1 tablespoon vegetable oil

8 spring onions (scallions), chopped into 5 cm (2 inch) lengths, plus extra, thinly sliced, to serve

200 g (7 oz) ginger, finely chopped

2 whole star anise

2 teaspoons Sichuan peppercorns

250 ml (9 fl oz/1 cup) dark soy sauce

2 tablespoons light soy sauce

125 ml (4 fl oz/½ cup) Shaoxing rice wine

2 tablespoons brown sugar or rock sugar (see Note)

1 tablespoon sea salt, or to taste

GINGER–SPRING ONION SAUCE

1 teaspoon sesame oil

½ teaspoon sugar

1 heaped tablespoon finely chopped ginger

60 g (2¼ oz/½ cup) finely chopped spring onions

1 teaspoon sea salt, or to taste

4 tablespoons vegetable oil

Remove the chicken from the refrigerator and bring to room temperature. Rinse and pat dry with paper towel.

To make a soy stock, heat the oil in a wok over medium heat, add the spring onions and ginger and stir-fry for 10 seconds or until fragrant. Transfer to a stockpot that holds 8–10 litres and add the remaining ingredients and 6 litres (210 fl oz/24 cups) water. Bring to the boil, then reduce heat to a simmer and cook for 15 minutes.

Carefully lower the chicken breast-side down into the stock. Simmer gently for 15 minutes, ensuring the stock doesn't boil, then remove from the heat, cover and leave for 40 minutes to finish cooking. To test if the chicken is cooked, pierce the thickest part of the thigh with a chopstick; if the juices run clear, it's ready. Remove the chicken from the stock and leave to cool, reserving the poaching liquid.

Meanwhile, for the ginger–spring onion sauce, blitz all the ingredients in a food processor until smooth. Season with salt and transfer to a serving bowl.

Chop the chicken Chinese-style (see Note) and arrange on a platter. Drizzle with a little poaching stock, garnish with spring onion, and serve with ginger–spring onion sauce.

Note *Rock sugar is available from Asian grocers. It needs to be crushed before using; the best way to do this is to put it in a snaplock bag and whack it with a meat mallet. To chop the chicken Chinese-style, use a cleaver to split the bird down the middle through the breastplate and backbone, then remove the legs and halve them at the joint. Remove and halve the wings in the same manner. Halve the breasts lengthways and cut into thick slices.*

Hainanese chicken rice

Here's some interesting news... while Hainanese chicken rice is practically the national dish of Singapore, this dish, made famous by my ancestors, is not that common in Hong Kong. Perhaps this has something to do with the relatively small Hainanese community in the city, but everyone I've spoken to knows of this legendary dish. It isn't difficult to make. You need a good free-range chicken and, after poaching the bird, the stock is used to steam the rice and to make the soup. The chicken is dressed and served with a dipping sauce. Where to find this delicious chicken in Hong Kong? As well as at Hainan Shaoye in Kowloon, it's on the menu of the Grand Café at the Grand Hyatt, Café Causette at the Mandarin Oriental, and Café Malacca over in Sai Wan.

In the time-honoured tradition, this recipe has been handed down from my mother and her mother before her.

1 x 1.8 kg (4 lb) free-range chicken
15 g (½ oz) ginger, bashed with the side of a knife
2 spring onions (scallions), chopped
1 bunch watercress, leaves picked
1 small cucumber, sliced crossways
Coriander (cilantro) sprigs, to serve (optional)

CHILLI SAUCE
6–8 long red chillies, chopped
20 g (¾ oz) ginger, sliced
4 garlic cloves
Juice of 2 limes
Chicken fat from the stock, to taste (optional)

RICE
5 red Asian shallots, thinly sliced
3 garlic cloves, finely chopped
600 g (1 lb 5 oz/3 cups) jasmine rice, rinsed
    and drained
2 pandan leaves, tied into a knot
875 ml (30 fl oz/3½ cups) chicken stock

DRESSING
2 tablespoons light soy sauce
½ teaspoon sesame oil
100 ml (3½ fl oz) chicken stock

Continued overleaf

Remove the pads of fat from the chicken cavity and reserve. Rub the chicken inside and out with 2 teaspoons salt. Loop cotton string around and under the wings and across the breast, then set aside for 30 minutes to come to room temperature.

Meanwhile, to make the chilli sauce, pound the ingredients except the lime juice with a mortar and pestle to a grainy paste (not too fine). Add the lime juice, season with salt and chicken fat to taste, if using, and mix well. Set aside.

Put the ginger, spring onions, 4 litres (140 fl oz/16 cups) water and 1 teaspoon salt in a large stockpot and bring to the boil. Holding the chicken by the string, lower it into the boiling stock, submerge for 60 seconds, then lift the chicken out, allowing the water to drain from the cavity. Repeat this a couple of times, bringing the stock back to the boil between each submersion. This process ensures the water circulating in the bird is hot enough for even cooking. Submerge the chicken again, bring the stock back to the boil, then reduce to a gentle simmer, cover and cook for 20 minutes.

Cover the pan with a lid, turn off the heat and leave the chicken for 40 minutes to finish cooking. Lift out the chicken, being careful not to break the skin. Let the stock drain from the cavity, then plunge the bird into a bath of iced water to stop cooking. Leave for 20 minutes, then remove, gently pat dry with paper towel and set aside. Reserve the chicken stock.

To prepare the rice, chop the reserved chicken fat and stir in a wok over medium heat until the fat renders, then discard the solids (or heat 2 tablespoons vegetable oil in a wok). Add the shallots and fry until golden, then add the garlic and fry for a further minute. Add the rice and fry until it begins to pop. Transfer to a saucepan (or a rice cooker). Add the pandan leaves and pour in the reserved hot stock to cover the rice by 2 cm (¾ inch). Increase the heat to high, bring to a simmer, then reduce heat to low, cover with a tightly fitting lid and cook until liquid is absorbed (11–12 minutes). Remove from the heat, remove lid, cover with a tea towel and leave for 5 minutes to steam dry.

Meanwhile, to make the dressing, combine the ingredients in a bowl.

To make the soup, add the watercress to the remaining stock. Adjust the seasoning with salt and white pepper.

Cut up the chicken Chinese-style (see Note) and arrange on a platter with the sliced cucumber. Pour the dressing over the chicken and garnish with coriander leaves, if using. Serve with separate bowls of rice and watercress broth and chilli sauce on the side.

Note *To chop the chicken Chinese-style, use a cleaver to split the bird down the middle through the breastplate and backbone, then remove the legs and halve them at the joint. Remove and halve the wings in the same manner. Halve the breasts lengthways and cut into thick slices.*

Sichuan tea-smoked duck

Serves 8

Said to have been invented by the kitchen brigade of the dowager empress of the Qing dynasty, Sichuan tea-smoked duck is one of the most-lauded Chinese delicacies.

This dish is far from difficult, but you need time and an old wok if you don't have a smoker. The bird is marinated, then steamed to render it tender before it's smoked on a bed of tea leaves. Finally, the duck is deep-fried to crisp the skin before it's presented to eager diners. I use duck legs and simmer them to save time. Start this recipe a day in advance.

8 duck legs
1 tablespoon sea salt
2 tablespoons Mei Kuei Lu Chiew
    (see Note) or Shaoxing rice wine
1 tablespoon Sichuan peppercorns
1 tablespoon fennel seeds
1 teaspoon cloves
5 spring onions (scallions), chopped
2–3 sticks cassia bark
2 whole star anise
1 walnut-sized piece ginger, crushed
Vegetable oil, for deep-frying

SICHUAN PEPPER–SALT DIP
1 tablespoon Sichuan peppercorns
4 tablespoons sea salt flakes

SMOKING INGREDIENTS
4 tablespoons tea leaves
150 g (5½ oz/¾ cup) rice
150 g (5½ oz/¾ cup) brown sugar

Put the duck legs in a bowl, prick with a fork and rub with salt. Splash Mei Kuei Lu or Shaoxing over the duck, mix well and leave to marinate for 2–3 hours.

Tie the Sichuan peppercorns, fennel seeds and cloves in a piece of muslin (cheesecloth) with string to form a bag. Put the bag and the spring onions, cassia bark, star anise and ginger in a large stockpot with 3 litres (105 fl oz/12 cups) water. Bring to the boil, then reduce the heat to simmer for about 15 minutes to allow the flavours to develop. Add the duck and simmer for 30–40 minutes until cooked through but not falling off the bone. Remove the pot from the heat and leave to cool, then refrigerate the duck in the stock for 12 hours.

To make the Sichuan pepper–salt dip, dry-roast the Sichuan peppercorns for 30 seconds in a hot pan, then transfer to a bowl. Add the sea salt flakes to the pan and stir continuously until golden. Add the salt to the peppercorns, cool and then grind finely in a spice grinder.

Pat the duck legs dry with paper towel. Line a large wok with a double layer of foil and put the smoking ingredients on top. Place the duck legs on a metal rack over the ingredients and cover tightly with the wok lid. Turn the heat to high and when smoke begins to escape put a damp cloth around the rim and reduce the heat to low. Leave to smoke for 10 minutes, then turn off the heat and leave for another 5 minutes. Remove the duck and discard the smoking ingredients.

Pat the duck dry with paper towel. Heat oil for deep-frying in the wok to 180°C (350°F) or until a piece of bread turns golden in 10 seconds. Deep-fry the duck legs until crisp and mahogany coloured. Serve warm with Sichuan pepper-salt dip and cucumber salad (page 46).

Note
Mei Kuei Lu Chiew liquor, a rose wine, is made with sorghum and rose petals. If it's unavailable, use Shaoxing rice wine.

Swiss chicken wings

Serves 4

Despite the name, these chicken wings bear no relation to Swiss food. They belong to the genre of 'Soy Sauce Western' food that's unique to Hong Kong. Combining Western technique or ingredients to suit the Chinese palate, this dish is a fine example of this hybridised cooking style from the 1950s and '60s. Apparently the name came about when a Western diner asked what this dish was called, to which the waiter replied 'sweet sauce'. And it eventually came to be known as 'Swiss' chicken wings. This dish is found in a number of casual Chinese eateries, including the much-loved Tai Ping Koon in Stanley Street in Central.

15 mid-section chicken wings (the section
   between the elbow and the tip)
250 ml (9 fl oz/1 cup) dark soy sauce
6 slices ginger
2 tablespoons Worcestershire sauce
2 whole star anise
100–200 g (3½–7 oz) rock sugar (see Note)
Chopped spring onions (scallions), to serve

Put the chicken wings in a saucepan, cover with cold water, bring to the boil, then tip into a colander and rinse under cold running water.

Place the soy sauce, ginger, Worcestershire sauce, star anise, sugar to taste and 250 ml (9 fl oz/1 cup) water in a saucepan. Bring to the boil, stirring until the sugar has dissolved. Add the chicken wings and simmer for 20 minutes or until the wings have taken on a dark hue. Transfer the chicken to a platter with a slotted spoon and simmer the sauce until reduced and thickened.

Pour the sauce over the chicken wings, garnish with spring onions and serve with steamed rice.

Note *Rock sugar is available from Asian grocers. It needs to be crushed before using; the best way to do this is to put it in a snaplock bag and whack it with a meat mallet.*

Peking duck

One of the world's great dishes, Peking duck always creates a sense of occasion. Amber-hued and aromatic with a gorgeous crisp skin and nuanced flavour, this is perhaps the dish that speaks the most of Chinese gastronomy. Carved at the table with pomp and ceremony, and wrapped in wafer-thin crêpes with spring onions, cucumber and hoisin sauce, Peking duck was apparently once served for the emperors of the Qing dynasty. But the cooks from the royal palaces left in the 19th century and the legendary duck made its way from Beijing to southern China.

I've eaten several versions of this grand dish. And watching Chinese chefs make it fills me with awe and admiration. To make an authentic version, Chinese chefs blow air through the neck of the duck to separate the skin from the meat. Then the bird is given a bath of maltose and vinegar before it's left to air-dry until the skin is like parchment. Finally, it's roasted in a traditional Chinese brick oven, hanging in an upright position on hooks, until it's glossy and crisp. Nowadays, Peking ducks are often roasted in a cylindrical oven similar to a tandoor. These commercial ovens are beyond the scope of most of us, but I have a couple of tips.

First, you need a large duck with unblemished skin and with the neck attached. If you wish to inflate the duck, you need a bicycle pump or a foot pump for exercise balls. Add marinade to the duck's cavity, then secure it with a bamboo skewer. Scald the skin with boiling water, ladle a seasoned vinegar-honey solution over the bird, then hang it from a meat hook in front of a fan and leave it to dry completely.

To roast the duck, if your oven is large enough, suspend it from a meat hook attached to the top rack and place a tray filled with water underneath to catch the fat. Otherwise, sit the duck on a wire rack set over a roasting tin filled with water. When it's done, cut up the duck and serve it with the traditional accompaniments.

This recipe is from Tang Court, the three Michelin-starred restaurant in the Langham Hotel in Tsim Sha Tsui. Traditionally in Hong Kong and China, only the skin is served with a crêpe, a smear of hoisin sauce, slices of cucumber and spring onion. The meat is then cut up and stir-fried with bean shoots to be served as a second course. This is what the Langham does. Nowadays, most restaurants carve the meat to serve with the skin.

P
O
U
L
T
R
Y

98

1 tablespoon sea salt

1 x 2.4 kg (5 lb 4 oz) duck

20 Mandarin pancakes (see Note)

100 ml (3½ fl oz) hoisin sauce, mixed with
    2 tablespoons Shaoxing rice wine

1 large cucumber, peeled and cut into 5 cm (2 inch)
    matchsticks

10 spring onions (scallions), white part only

MARINADE

50 g (1¾ oz) ginger, finely chopped

50 g (1¾ oz) spring onions (scallions), thinly sliced

2 whole star anise

2 teaspoons Chinese five-spice

60 g (2¼ oz) sea salt

GLAZE

50 g (1¾ oz) maltose or honey

100 ml (3½ fl oz) red rice vinegar

30 ml (1 fl oz) clear rice vinegar

1 tablespoon light soy sauce

1 tablespoon dark soy sauce

250 ml (9 fl oz/1 cup) hot water

Rub the sea salt all over the duck, rinse and pat dry with paper towel. Mix the marinade ingredients in a bowl, then rub the marinade inside the cavity of the duck. Secure the cavity with a bamboo or metal skewer.

Use a bicycle pump to blow up the skin from the neck end until the duck inflates. Secure the neck firmly with kitchen string to prevent the air escaping (you can skip this step). Pour boiling water all over the duck to tighten the skin.

Heat the glaze ingredients in a saucepan, stirring well, then brush the glaze all over the duck until it's a tan colour.

Using a meat hook or kitchen string, hang the duck in a draughty place (such as under the kitchen rangehood) for at least 8 hours or until the skin is taut and as dry as parchment. Use an electric fan to speed up the drying process. Do not prick the skin at any stage.

Preheat the oven to 220°C (425°F). Place the duck on a wire rack set over a roasting tin filled with water and roast for 15 minutes, then reduce the heat to 180°C (350°F) and roast for a further 40–45 minutes until cooked through.

Leave the duck to rest for 3–5 minutes, then carve it and serve with steamed Mandarin pancakes, hoisin sauce, cucumber and spring onion.

Note *Mandarin pancakes are available from Asian grocers.*

Braised abalone and chicken with sand ginger

Man Wah in the classy Mandarin Oriental Hotel is like a Chinese lacquered box. With its refined interiors and views over Victoria Harbour, this Cantonese restaurant evokes an atmosphere of a bygone era when life was genteel and food was crafted with love. For this reason, it's my sentimental favourite in Hong Kong. On my last visit, I had a delicious dish of braised abalone and chicken with sand ginger. Intrigued, I asked to speak with chef Hung Chi Kwong, who told me sand ginger is essential for this dish. Also known as resurrection lily, aromatic ginger, *kencur* and *cekur*, this member of the ginger family has distinctive scents of pepper and camphor. It's sold dried or ground in Asian grocers, so I've adapted chef Hung's recipe and used ground rather than fresh.

3 x 70 g (2½ oz) baby abalone
   (see Note), preferably live
200 g (7 oz) boned chicken thighs,
   cut into bite-sized pieces
500 ml (17 fl oz/2 cups) vegetable oil
30 g (1 oz) ginger, finely chopped
125 ml (4 fl oz/½ cup) chicken stock
1 teaspoon light soy sauce
½ teaspoon dark soy sauce
1 teaspoon oyster sauce
1 teaspoon cornflour (cornstarch),
   mixed with 1 tablespoon water

20 g (¾ oz) Chinese celery, finely
   chopped
2 teaspoons goji berries, soaked
   in 125 ml (4 fl oz/½ cup) water
   until plump (optional)

MARINADE
1 tablespoon light soy sauce
½ teaspoon sugar
1 tablespoon Shaoxing rice wine
1 teaspoon ground sand ginger

Put the abalone in a steamer on a saucepan of simmering water over medium heat, cover and steam for 20 minutes. Cool, then, using a tablespoon, remove each abalone from its shell, cut off the liver and the frilly skirt and scrub clean.

Meanwhile, combine the marinade ingredients and a pinch of salt in a bowl, add the chicken, mix well and leave to marinate for 10 minutes.

Heat the oil in a wok to 170°C (325°F) or until a piece of bread turns golden in 10 seconds. Carefully slide the cleaned abalone into the hot oil and fry for 30 seconds. Remove with a slotted spoon and drain on paper towel. When cool enough to handle, slice lengthways into 1 cm (½ inch) strips.

In the same oil, fry the marinated chicken for 30 seconds, then remove with a slotted spoon and drain on paper towel.

Pour the oil into a heatproof container (reserve for another use), leaving 1 tablespoon in the wok. Return the wok to high heat and stir-fry the ginger until fragrant. Return the chicken and abalone to the wok and add the stock, soy sauces and oyster sauce. Reduce to medium heat and cook for 3–4 minutes.

Check the seasoning, adjust with salt and white pepper and stir in the cornflour mixture to thicken the sauce. Add the celery and goji berries and serve.

Note *If fresh abalone isn't available, frozen abalone is sold in select fish shops and Asian supermarkets.*

Stir-fried chicken with lap cheong and snow peas

Serves 2-4

I love snow peas for their crunchy texture, and this super-easy dish is one of my favourite ways to serve them. This recipe uses chicken, but it also works well with prawns or calamari. Just don't omit the lap cheong – it takes this home-style dish to another dimension.

1 tablespoon vegetable oil
2 garlic cloves, thinly sliced
1 slice ginger
200 g (7 oz) chicken thigh fillets, thinly sliced
1 lap cheong sausage, thinly sliced
1 tablespoon Shaoxing rice wine
250 g (9 oz) snow peas (mangetouts), trimmed
1 tablespoon oyster sauce
100 ml (3½ fl oz) chicken stock
½ teaspoon sesame oil

Put the oil into a hot wok, add the garlic and ginger and stir-fry for 20 seconds. Add the chicken and lap cheong and stir-fry until the chicken starts to colour. Deglaze the pan with the Shaoxing rice wine, then add the snow peas, oyster sauce and chicken stock.

Increase the heat to high and cook until the snow peas are just tender. Check the seasoning and adjust with salt and white pepper, drizzle with sesame oil and serve with steamed rice.

My chicken bao

Makes 10

This recipe is inspired by an incredible dish I enjoyed at Little Bao, an edgy diner conceived by chef May Chow, and one of the hottest places to dine in Hong Kong. May is a friend and one helluva talented chef. She was named Asia's Best Female Chef 2017 by Asia's 50 Best Restaurants, an offshoot of the World's 50 Best Restaurants awards. May presents her bao like a hamburger. My version is shaped like a *gua bao*, a Chinese sandwich-style steamed bun. I've given the recipe for these buns below, or they can be found in the freezer section of Asian grocers.

500 g (1 lb 2 oz) boned chicken
    thighs, cut into 5 cm (2 inch)
    strips
2 eggs, beaten
300 g (10½ oz/2 cups) plain
    (all-purpose) flour mixed with
    1 teaspoon salt
Oil, for deep-frying
1 large handful basil
1 large handful coriander (cilantro)

PICKLED CARROT
250 ml (9 fl oz/1 cup) white rice
    vinegar
100 g (3½ oz) sugar
200 g (7 oz) julienned carrots

MARINADE
1 tablespoon light soy sauce
½ teaspoon Chinese five-spice
½ teaspoon chilli powder
½ teaspoon salt, to taste
½ teaspoon white pepper
1 teaspoon cornflour (cornstarch)

SICHUAN MAYONNAISE
1 tablespoon Sichuan pepper oil
200 ml (7 fl oz) Kewpie mayonnaise

BAO DOUGH
½ quantity bao dough (see char siu
    bao page 202)
Vegetable oil, for brushing

To make the pickled carrot, simmer the vinegar, sugar, 125 ml (4 fl oz/½ cup) water and 1 teaspoon salt in a small saucepan, stirring until the sugar dissolves. Cool completely, then add the carrots and refrigerate overnight.

Combine the marinade ingredients in a bowl, add the chicken and stir to coat. Cover the bowl with plastic wrap and refrigerate for at least 2 hours or overnight.

To make the Sichuan mayonnaise, combine the ingredients and set aside.

To make the *gua bao*, roll the dough into a cylinder and cut into 10 pieces. Roll each into a ball, then flatten with the palm of your hand. Sprinkle with flour and roll each into a 15 cm (6 inch) oval. Brush with oil, fold in half and press gently. Place on squares of baking paper and leave to prove until doubled in size (about 1 hour). Steam the buns in batches in a steamer until puffed (8–10 minutes).

Meanwhile, combine the beaten eggs and 125 ml (4 fl oz/½ cup) water in a bowl. Place the seasoned flour in a shallow bowl. Dip the chicken pieces in the eggwash, then the flour, shaking off the excess.

Heat oil in a deep-fryer or wok to 180°C (350°C) or until a piece of bread browns in 10 seconds, and deep-fry the chicken in batches until golden and crisp. Remove with a slotted spoon and drain on paper towel. When all the chicken is done, deep-fry the basil for a couple of seconds until crisp. Drain on paper towel.

To serve, stuff the chicken pieces into the split bao with carrots, fried basil and coriander, and top with mayonnaise.

P
O
U
L
T
R
Y

106

seafood

AT ELEVEN IN THE MORNING ON A HOT HONG KONG SUNDAY THE FERRY RIDE TO LAMMA ISLAND IS CROWDED.

It's packed with day-trippers and residents heading back to the car-free island after a night of revelry in the city. As the ferry approaches the jetty of the sleepy fishing village of Sok Kwu Wan, the Hong Kong most visitors know seems a million miles away.

I've been brought here by Angela Li, best known in Hong Kong's cultural world for her art gallery in Sheung Wan. An internationally recognised authority on contemporary Chinese art, Angela is also a gastronome. And the reason we're here is to eat at the alfresco seafood restaurants that line the waterfront. Well-known among hard-core food lovers for serving some of the finest (yet fairly inexpensive) seafood outside Hong Kong proper, the restaurants here offer pristine fish from the local fish farm, supplemented by seafood from around the world.

The cooking style at these mostly family-run places is Cantonese. As we look through the tanks filled with live sea bream, tilapia, garoupa, sea snails, phallic-looking geoduck and prehistoric-looking mantis prawns, the seasoned waiter makes recommendations for how to cook our selections. Pretty soon, expertly cooked plump scallops with the merest hint of ginger arrive with slippery glass noodles, along with sweet clams with black beans and chillies.

When the platter of typhoon shelter-style mantis prawns is placed on the table, our conversation pauses. Dropped in smoking hot oil, the crustaceans' shells have been shocked into crisp deliciousness by the intense heat. In the process, the shells have been separated and the meat remains tender. Topped with a mountain of crisp golden fried garlic, chillies and spring onions, this dish is a showstopper.

As we tuck into these insanely delicious prawns, eating with our fingers, Angela gives me a lesson on seafood appreciation and why it's such an obsession with Hong Kong people. To begin with, the Cantonese word for seafood is 'hoi sin', which loosely means fresh things or offerings from the sea, and, of course, the fresher the seafood, the better it tastes. Any seafood that's a couple of days old is shunned. Chefs and seafood buffs insist on live seafood to capture that freshness. Hence, no self-respecting seafood restaurant would fail to feature tanks of live seafood at its entrance. In high-end restaurants, where there are no seafood tanks on display, a live fish in a basket is brought to the diner for viewing before it's dispatched in the kitchen.

There's also a cultural significance to eating fish. In Chinese, the word for fish is 'yu'. Pronounced with a different accent, it also means abundance and affluence. So the more fish that is eaten, the more benefits one will receive.

Furthermore, Chinese people love eating a whole fish. This relates to the Chinese philosophical belief that life has a beginning and an end. I'm no Chinese sage, but I'm more than happy to eat the belly, the fins, tail and all.

The usual method for cooking super-fresh fish is steaming, because the moisture seals in the flavour. Taking a matter of minutes, this method is foolproof, but it pays to bear a few details in mind. You need to consider the variety of fish you wish to steam. Oily fish, for instance, doesn't take well to steaming. Know your fish and consider the size, and you'll be able to determine the time it will take to steam it to perfection.

Steamed with ginger, soy sauces, sesame oil, sugar and sometimes rice wine, and topped with a shower of coriander and spring onions, a whole fish is finished with a splash of hot oil in a classic Cantonese method that makes for sensational eating. Those who know a thing or two about eating fish will immediately go for the tender cheeks.

On one occasion, I was taken to Po Toi Island with my friends Paul and Diane Tighe, whose knowledge of all things culinary on the south side of Hong Kong Island is quite remarkable. Accessible only by ferry either from Stanley or Aberdeen, this tiny outcrop is famous for two things: hiking and a casual restaurant serving the most divine seafood. Located in the sheltered cove, Ming Kee Restaurant's party atmosphere attracts well-heeled pleasure-seekers, who arrive in company junks and yachts for the weekend.

In its massive kitchen, vats of live fish, crayfish, crab and prawns await their fate. We order prawns by the catty, the Chinese unit of measurement. Prepared Cantonese-style with a reduction of soy sauce, sugar and Shaoxing rice wine, this classic dish of twice-cooked prawns is splendid (page 128). Perhaps it has something to do with the sun and the gentle sea breeze or the Tsingtao beer, but a lobster with e-fu noodles scented with garlic and ginger will be in my memory forever.

To say seafood cookery in Hong Kong is extraordinary and eclectic is an understatement. Perhaps this has something to do with the city's cosmopolitan nature, but I nearly fell off my perch when goose-neck barnacles, the prized delicacy the folks of Galicia would risk their lives for, was presented to me by David Lai, one of the city's top Western-trained chefs. Equally breathtaking is the deep-fried stuffed crab from the Four Seasons (page 134) cooked by Chan Yan Tak, who has the distinction of being the first Chinese chef to earn three Michelin stars. On the traditional front, chef Kwong Wai Keong's lobster with a trio of alliums, served at three Michelin-starred T'ang Court, is outstanding.

European-trained chefs have also contributed to the seafood scene. At Arcane, the chic restaurant helmed by multi-award-winning chef Shane Osborn, the seasonal menu features seafood of exceptional quality. His kingfish carpaccio with jicama and fennel (page 118) is drool-worthy. As for Richard Ekkebus, chef at Amber Restaurant, currently placed 24th on the World's 50 Best Restaurants list, his signature Hokkaido sea urchin dish (page 130) is sublime.

The modest collection of recipes in this chapter is only skimming the surface of the seafood scene of this vibrant city. I definitely think it's time you paid a visit.

Cantonese lobster with spring onion, shallots and red onion

Cantonese chef Kwong Wai Keung, who heads up the three Michelin-starred T'ang Court Restaurant in the Langham Hotel, is revered by his peers and known for executing some of the most beautiful Chinese cooking in Hong Kong. This lobster dish is a revelation. Marrying members of the humble onion family with luxe lobster is a stroke of genius and the result is incredibly delicious. The lobster is deep-fried briefly to seal in the flavour, then, in the same oil, a sliced onion is cooked with the Chinese technique called *guo you*, meaning 'waving through the oil'. It's very much a restaurant practice, but skipping this step and stir-frying the onion instead doesn't make a huge difference at home. If you like to spoil yourself and your loved ones, this dish will do it.

1 x 800 g (1 lb 12 oz) live lobster
Vegetable oil, for deep-frying
3 red Asian shallots, about 120 g
    (4¼ oz), thinly sliced
1 red onion, about 120 g (4¼ oz),
    thinly sliced
5 spring onions (scallions), white
    part only, cut into 5 cm
    (2 inch) lengths
1 garlic clove, finely chopped

A splash of Shaoxing rice wine,
    to deglaze the pan
Thinly sliced spring onions
    (scallions), to garnish

SAUCE
250 ml (9 fl oz/1 cup) Shaoxing
    rice wine
2 tablespoons light soy sauce
½ teaspoon sugar

Kill the lobster humanely by placing it in the freezer for a couple of hours to put it to sleep, then placing it on its back and splitting it swiftly with a sharp knife. Chop the tail section in half lengthways and remove the intestinal tract. Cut each half section into bite-sized pieces across the shell. Discard the head (unless you like to deep-fry it for presentation).

Heat the oil in a wok or deep-fryer to 170°C (325°F) or until a cube of bread turns golden in 10 seconds, and deep-fry the shallots until just golden (5–8 minutes). Transfer to a sieve with a slotted spoon to drain, then transfer to a plate lined with paper towel.

Add the sliced onion to the same oil for 5 seconds and remove with a slotted spoon. Drain and set aside.

Increase the heat of the oil to 190°C (375°F) and deep-fry the lobster in batches until the shell turns red. Remove and drain on paper towel.

For the sauce, combine the ingredients in a small bowl.

Carefully pour the oil into a heatproof container (reserve for another use), leaving 1 tablespoon in the wok. Add the spring onion and garlic and stir-fry briefly until aromatic, then return the lobster to the wok. Deglaze the wok with a splash of Shaoxing. Return the onion to the wok and add the sauce. Cook over medium heat until the sauce thickens and coats the lobster. Transfer to a serving plate and shower with the crisp shallots and spring onions before serving.

Steamed crab claw with egg white custard

Serves 1

High up in the clouds, in the world's tallest hotel, is one of Hong Kong's culinary jewels. With its soaring floor-to-ceiling windows, the luxe Tin Lung Heen in the swanky Ritz-Carlton is definitely a restaurant for a special occasion. Awarded two Michelin stars since it opened in 2011, the restaurant is helmed by Paul Lee, a Cantonese chef with an incredible reputation. And chef Lee certainly knows a thing or two about seafood, as demonstrated by this dish of steamed crab claw. One of the most highly prized seafoods in the region, mud crab is sweet and delicate, and eating a single perfectly steamed crab claw set over a quivering egg custard is a revelation.

80 g (2¾ oz) egg white
Pinch of sugar, to taste
3½ tablespoons chicken stock or superior stock
    (see page 241)
1 x 75 g (2¾ oz) shelled fresh crab claw
1 tablespoon Shaoxing rice wine
1 teaspoon potato flour, mixed with
    2 tablespoons water
Coriander (cilantro) leaves, to garnish

Whisk together the egg white, sugar, a pinch of salt and 1½ tablespoons chicken stock with chopsticks or a fork. Strain the mixture into a serving bowl, place in a steamer over a pan of simmering water, cover and steam for 2–3 minutes or until just set. Keep the custard warm.

Put the crab claw and Shaoxing rice wine in a small pan, place in a steamer over a saucepan of simmering water, cover and steam for 3–4 minutes until just firm.

Strain the steaming juices from the crab into a small saucepan and add the remaining chicken stock. Bring the sauce to the boil and thicken with the potato flour mixture.

Arrange the crab on the steamed custard and pour the sauce over the top. Garnish with coriander and serve.

精美小食

香脆油條	12	香煎蘿蔔糕	$14
郊外油菜	$14	炸雞翼(3隻)	$18
五香咸肉粽	$17	炸魚皮	$25
香煎墨魚餅(3件)	$25	時菜灼雙菇	$22
芥鯪魚球	$35	潮式煎蠔餅	$35
炸雲吞	$35	原汁牛腩	$50
乳豬手	$50	五香牛肚	$50
薑蔥灼鮮牛肉	$50	薑蔥灼豬肝	$50
薑蔥撈雲吞(6粒)	$25	薑蔥撈水餃	$28
薑蔥撈水餃(5粒)	$28	雞翼(3隻)	$18
		豬腰	$50

Kingfish carpaccio with jicama, fennel confit, soy and ginger

Serves 4

Shane Osborn was the first Australian chef to be awarded two Michelin stars when he worked at London's Pied à Terre. He gave it all away to spend time with his young family. Enticed to Hong Kong to helm the short-lived St Betty, this incredibly talented chef went on to open Arcane, a sleek contemporary restaurant in Central. He creates magic with seasonal ingredients and presents them in the most uncluttered and relaxed Aussie style. His menu is concise and ingeniously simple, and this carpaccio with jicama salad, fennel confit and an Asian-inspired dressing is a fine example. While other chefs of his calibre frequently strut the world stage, this laconic and quietly passionate man is usually seen in his favourite spot – his kitchen. You'll love this recipe. It's refreshing and ever so light and, as a bonus, everything can be made in advance. The original recipe uses hamachi or yellowtail kingfish, but any fresh white-fleshed fish works well.

120 g (4¼ oz) jicama (see Note), finely chopped
250 g (9 oz) kingfish, thinly sliced
Sea salt, to taste
Micro coriander (coriander) and shiso, to garnish
1 tablespoon toasted sesame seeds (optional)
Dill, to garnish

FENNEL CONFIT
2 small fennel bulbs
500 ml (17 fl oz/2 cups) extra virgin olive oil
2 whole star anise

SOY AND GINGER DRESSING
3 tablespoons white balsamic
½ teaspoon lemon juice
1 teaspoon yuzu juice
1 tablespoon light soy sauce
1 teaspoon lemon oil
1 teaspooon sesame oil
2 teaspoons finely grated ginger
160 ml (5¼ fl oz) extra virgin olive oil

To make the fennel confit, cut the fennel into 5 mm (¼ inch) dice and put into a saucepan with the extra virgin olive oil, star anise and a pinch of salt. Cook over low heat until the fennel is tender but still firm (15–20 minutes). Leave to cool in the oil.

Drain the fennel and put 150 g (5½ oz) in a bowl with the jicama. Season well with salt and pepper and mix well.

Arrange the sliced kingfish on a plate. Season lightly with sea salt, spread the jicama and fennel over the top and sprinkle with micro coriander and shiso. Mix together the dressing ingredients, season with salt and spoon 4 tablespoons of dressing over everything (reserve the remainder for another use; it will keep for a week). Finish with a sprinkling of sesame seeds.

Note *Jicama, a root vegetable also known as yam bean, is available from Asian grocers.*

Cantonese-style steamed fish

In Hong Kong diners expect their seafood to be super-fresh, which is why you find so many fish tanks on display in Chinese restaurants. Steaming is the favourite cooking method – it retains the sweet 'sea freshness', a term commonly used by the Chinese to describe the intrinsic flavour of seafood. The fish is often seasoned with soy sauce and then, when it's cooked, spring onions are scattered on top and given a splash of hot oil, which partially cooks them and releases their fragrance and flavour. Traditionally, a whole fish is used for this recipe because it represents the beginning (the head) and end (the tail) of a story. You can always steam fillets of fish if you prefer.

1 x 1 kg (2 lb 4 oz) whole barramundi, scaled and
   gutted, or 500 g (1 lb 2 oz) fish fillets
2 tablespoons julienned ginger
2 tablespoons light soy sauce
1 teaspoon dark soy sauce
2 teaspoons sesame oil
½ teaspoon caster (superfine) sugar
4 spring onions (scallions), julienned
2 tablespoons peanut oil
1 handful coriander, to garnish

Pat the cleaned fish dry with paper towel and make two diagonal slashes on each side. Rub salt all over the fish, including in the cavity. Place the fish in a heatproof dish and spread the ginger evenly over the top. Leave for 10 minutes.

Place a steamer or a wire rack in a wok or deep pan. Fill the wok or pan with water to just below the steamer or rack and bring to the boil. Mix the soy sauces, sesame oil and sugar, and pour this mixture over the fish. Place the dish on the rack and cover with a lid. Steam over high heat for 8–12 minutes (depending on the circulation of steam in the wok) until the fish flakes easily.

Carefully remove the plate from the steamer. Transfer the fish to a heated serving platter and pour the sauce from the steaming plate over the fish. Scatter the spring onions over the fish. Heat the peanut oil in a small saucepan until smoking and pour it over the spring onions. Serve immediately.

Curry fish balls

If you ever walk the crowded streets of Hong Kong, especially around Mong Kok, you'll probably catch the whiff of curry fish balls. Much loved by students after class or locals wanting an instant fix, curry fish balls are a popular snack because they're affordable and ubiquitous. They're usually sold near train stations where foot traffic is plentiful. You can also find them in the Temple Street Night Market. I often serve them with steamed rice as a light lunch, but most Hong Kong diners enjoy them on their own. Fish balls are simple to make, but they're also readily available from the refrigerator section of Asian grocers. I've included a recipe for them; if you use bought, you need 20 for this recipe.

3 tablespoons vegetable oil
1 small brown onion, finely chopped
2 garlic cloves, finely chopped
3 tablespoons mild curry powder,
    mixed with 2 tablespoons water
1 teaspoon chilli powder (optional)
1 litre (35 fl oz/4 cups) chicken stock
1 tablespoon light soy sauce
1 teaspoon sugar
125 ml (4 fl oz/½ cup) evaporated
    milk

½ teaspoon sesame oil
1 teaspoon cornflour (cornstarch),
    mixed with 2 tablespoons water

FISH BALLS
500 g (1 lb 2 oz) white fish fillets,
    cut into small pieces, with no
    skin or bone
2 egg whites
1 tablespoon cornflour (cornstarch)
1 teaspoon sugar

To make the fish balls, blend the fish in a food processor for 30 seconds or until paste-like. Add the remaining ingredients, 3 tablespoons water and salt and pepper, and blend for 2 minutes, stopping to scrape down the sides. Blend for another 3 minutes until well mixed.

Transfer the paste to a large bowl. Gather a handful of paste and slap it against the side of the bowl about 30 times until the mixture is glossy. This creates the 'bouncy' texture of the fish balls.

With wet hands, shape the paste into balls. Drop them into a saucepan of boiling water. As soon as they float, remove them with a slotted spoon.

Heat the oil in a saucepan. Add the onion and fry for 30 seconds, then lower the heat, add the garlic and fry until fragrant. Add the curry powder and chilli powder and stir-fry for 1–2 minutes, or until aromatic. Add the chicken stock, soy sauce, sugar, evaporated milk and sesame oil, bring to the boil and add the fish balls. Reduce to a simmer and cook, stirring occasionally, for 8–10 minutes. Stir in the cornflour mixture to thicken the sauce. Check the seasoning and serve.

Note *If you want to freeze fish balls, cool them completely and pack them into freezer bags. Use within a month.*

Stir-fried pipis with XO sauce

Serves 2-4

A *dai pai dong* translates as a 'stall with a big licence plate'. These licences were issued after the Second World War to families of civil servants who were killed or disabled, allowing them to open restaurants in the streets to make a living. Serving incredibly cheap and delicious food, these outdoor eateries quickly became places for locals to socialise. They reached their peak in the 1950s but because of noise and traffic complaints they were moved to food centres. Today some 30 original *dai pai dong* licences are left. The affection for these original casual eateries, however, is such that now the term *dai pai dong* is used for any outdoor casual eating place. I've eaten glorious thin-shelled clams with savoury XO sauce many times in such places and this recipe is my take on those memorable experiences.

2 tablespoons vegetable oil
2 garlic cloves, finely chopped
2 tablespoons julienned ginger
1 kg (2 lb 4 oz) small pipis
3 tablespoons XO sauce (see page 248)
3 tablespoons Shaoxing rice wine
3 tablespoons chicken stock
1 tablespoon light soy sauce
½ teaspoon dark soy sauce
½ teaspoon sugar
2 spring onions (scallions), cut into
    5 cm (2 inch) lengths
1 long red chilli, seeded and thinly sliced

Heat the oil in a wok. When hot, add the garlic and ginger and stir-fry for 15 seconds or until fragrant. Add the pipis and XO sauce, give them a good toss, then add the Shaoxing rice wine, chicken stock, soy sauces and sugar. Stir to combine and bring to the boil. Cover with a lid and cook, removing the pipis as they open. Add the spring onions and chilli to the sauce, then pour the sauce over the pipis. Serve with steamed rice or mantou buns to mop up the sauce.

Note *Depending on where the pipis were harvested, they can be very salty, so be judicious with seasoning. The length of time it takes for pipis to open depends on their size.*

Steamed oysters with black bean sauce

The ubiquitous black bean sauce has had a less-than-flattering reputation for being gloopy but, if made properly, this sauce is a beauty. It's especially delicious with seafood, and when paired with dried tangerine peel it lifts the flavour of seafood to a different realm. Matched with oysters, this combination is divine. I've had some really good renditions of this classic in Hong Kong, but this recipe from chef Anthony Lui of Flower Drum in Melbourne is just as good. Chef Lui first makes a black bean-tangerine sauce, then he makes a second sauce to pour over the black bean sauce after the oysters are steamed. Ingenious!

24 oysters, on the half-shell
1 large handful coriander (cilantro)
Finely chopped spring onions
   (scallions), to garnish

1 tablespoon Shaoxing rice wine
2 tablespoons chicken stock, mixed
   with ¼ teaspoon cornflour
   (cornstarch)
2 teaspoons sugar

BLACK BEAN SAUCE
3 tablespoons fermented black beans
1 piece dried tangerine peel
1 tablespoon vegetable oil
3 cm (1¼ inch) ginger,
   finely chopped
2 small garlic cloves, finely chopped
1 tablespoon oyster sauce
½ teaspoon dark soy sauce

SECOND SAUCE
300 ml (10½ fl oz) chicken stock
1 tablespoon Shaoxing rice wine
1 tablespoon oyster sauce
3 teaspoons light soy sauce
½ teaspoon dark soy sauce
Pinch of sugar

To make the black bean sauce, soak the fermented black beans and tangerine peel in warm water in separate bowls for about 15 minutes or until soft, then drain. Tear the tangerine peel into small pieces and blend with the black beans in a mini food processor or finely chop by hand. Transfer the mixture to a bowl, cover with plastic wrap and steam over simmering water for 30 minutes. Set aside to cool.

   Heat the vegetable oil in a small saucepan over medium heat, add the ginger and garlic and fry for a minute, then add the black bean mixture and remaining ingredients. Stir well and simmer for 30 seconds. Adjust the seasoning and remove from the heat.

   To make the second sauce, bring the ingredients to the boil in a small saucepan, stirring to combine. Simmer for 2 minutes, then keep warm.

   Spoon ½ teaspoon black bean sauce onto each oyster. Put the oysters in a steamer set on a saucepan of simmering water over medium heat, cover and steam for 3–4 minutes or until just cooked (oysters are cooked when the texture is firm to the touch).

   Transfer the oysters to serving plates. Spoon the warm second sauce over the oysters, sprinkle with coriander and spring onions and serve at once.

Cantonese twice-cooked prawns with soy sauce

Serves 6

Offered in most Cantonese restaurants in Hong Kong, this simple but sophisticated dish will test your wok skills. It looks deceptively easy and straightforward, but there are a couple of pointers to bear in mind. It's best to deep-fry the prawns until they are partially cooked. By doing this, the prawn shells take on a distinctive fragrance. The other point to remember is that timing is everything here – have all the ingredients ready or mixed so the prawns aren't overcooked and will remain succulent. Should you decide not to deep-fry the prawns, you can omit this step and stir-fry them instead.

Vegetable oil, for deep-frying
12 large prawns, unpeeled, but deveined
    (see Note), at room temperature
1–2 tablespoons finely chopped spring onion (scallion)

SAUCE
1½ teaspoons light soy sauce
¾ teaspoon dark soy sauce
3 tablespoons Shaoxing rice wine
2 teaspoons sugar, or to taste

To make the sauce, stir together the ingredients and set aside.

Heat vegetable oil in a wok over high heat to 240°C (475°F). Add the prawns in batches and deep-fry until the shells turn red. Remove with a slotted spoon and drain on paper towel. Discard the oil.

Return the wok to medium–high heat, add 1 tablespoon oil, then the prawns and sauce. Stir-fry for 30 seconds and serve hot with spring onion.

Note *To devein an unpeeled prawn, bend the prawn and use a fine skewer to pierce the shell and tease out the vein.*

Sea urchin in lobster jelly with cauliflower and caviar

A favourite among chefs and food lovers alike, Amber is one of the Hong Kong restaurants that I return to every year. A beautifully appointed, luxurious space, it delivers some of the best food and wine experiences not only in Hong Kong, but anywhere in the world. Serving contemporary French with Asian notes, Amber is the only establishment in the city to join the ranks of the élite World's 50 Best Restaurants. This is thanks to Dutch-born chef and culinary director Richard Ekkebus, whose passion for his craft is infectious and humbling. I've spent several happy hours talking food with this talented and gentle chef. When I told him about my book, chef Ekkebus happily shared this signature dish of sea urchin with lobster jelly and cauliflower mousse. It's wildly sublime. This is a restaurant dish requiring some exquisite ingredients and techniques; however, it is achievable. Chef Ekkebus uses Hokkaido sea urchin that is flown in daily to this trading hub, but any fresh sea urchin will do. He also uses titanium-strength gelatine sheets. He serves this dish with a crisp seaweed waffle.

6 sea urchins
40 g (1½ oz) caviar (chef Ekkebus
    uses oscietra or farmed kaluga
    schrenckii)
1 edible gold leaf
Coarse sea salt or ice, for serving

CAULIFLOWER MOUSSE
500 g (1 lb 2 oz) cauliflower, cut
    into small pieces
100 g (3½ oz) butter
1 litre (35 fl oz/4 cups) milk
Fine sea salt, to taste
2 titanium-strength gelatine sheets,
    soaked in iced water
400 ml (14 fl oz) single cream

LOBSTER CONSOMMÉ
1 tablespoon olive oil
500 g (1 lb 2 oz) rock lobster, split
    in two and cut into 8 pieces
1 vine-ripened tomato, chopped
½ celery stalk, peeled and diced
1 white onion, finely chopped
1 tablespoon brandy
250 ml (9 fl oz/1 cup) dry white wine
1 litre (35 fl oz/4 cups) chicken stock
2 titanium-strength gelatine sheets,
    soaked in iced water

S
E
A
F
O
O
D

Continued overleaf

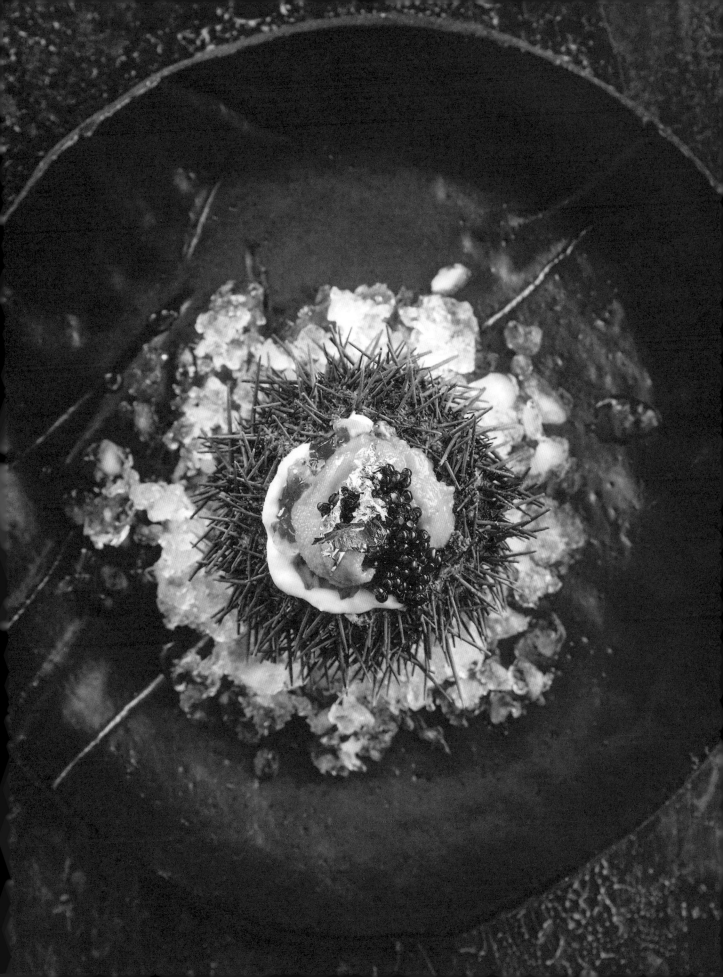

Neatly cut open the sea urchins with scissors, carefully remove the fingers of roe (which resemble tongues) with a teaspoon and refrigerate. Clean the shells, rinse and dry well and refrigerate.

To make the cauliflower mousse, gently sauté the cauliflower in the butter until glazed but not coloured. Add the milk and a pinch of salt. Boil the cauliflower in the milk until softened. Process the cauliflower mixture in a blender until smooth, then pass the purée through a sieve.

Warm 100 g (3½ oz) cauliflower purée in a small heavy-based saucepan, then remove from the heat. Add the gelatine and stir until dissolved, then add another 300 g (10½ oz) of cauliflower purée and mix well. Cool over ice until the gelatine starts to set. Meanwhile, whip the cream to soft peaks with a pinch of salt. Gently fold into the remaining cauliflower purée, then gently fold in the cauliflower–gelatine mixture. Check the seasoning and add salt if necessary. Spoon the cauliflower mousse into a piping bag and refrigerate until required.

To make the lobster consommé, heat the olive oil in a heavy-based saucepan over medium heat, add the lobster and fry until golden brown. Add the tomato, celery and onion, sauté gently until the juices have evaporated, then deglaze the pan with brandy and flambé until the alcohol has burned off. Add the wine and simmer to reduce to a syrupy consistency. Add the chicken stock to just cover and bring to a simmer, skimming the impurities off the surface. Keep the stock just under boiling point and simmer gently for 20 minutes, skimming the surface occasionally to achieve a clear bouillon. Leave to cool for 30 minutes.

Pass the bouillon through a sieve lined with rinsed muslin (cheesecloth) into a clean saucepan. Simmer the bouillon to reduce slightly and concentrate the flavours. Measure 1 litre (35 fl oz/4 cups) of the bouillon and reheat (reserve the remainder for another use). Squeeze the excess water from the gelatine and dissolve in the bouillon. Check the seasoning and add salt if necessary. Cool over a bowl of ice until the bouillon starts to set.

Set aside the 20 best-looking sea urchin tongues. Divide the remainder of the tongues among the shells, spoon cauliflower mousse on top of each and smooth into a dome shape. Neatly arrange the reserved tongues on each, then refrigerate for 1 hour to set. Top each with 2 tablespoons of almost-set lobster consommé jelly and refrigerate again for 1 hour until firm.

To serve, arrange the sea urchin shells on shaved ice or salt, top each with a small spoonful of caviar and, using tweezers, garnish each with a little gold leaf.

Deep-fried stuffed crab

This recipe is from Lung King Heen, a contemporary Cantonese restaurant hidden away in a quiet corner of the luxurious Four Seasons Hotel. In 2009 it became the first Cantonese restaurant in the world to win three Michelin stars. This achievement is down to the dedication of chef Chan Yan Tak, who was lured out of retirement to head this elegant restaurant. His cooking is exquisite and his loyal team is one of the most dedicated I've come across. His dim sum are works of art and, unlike at so many other establishments, they're steamed individually to order. Incredibly self-effacing, he explains this deceptively simple recipe is all about quality ingredients, heat control and timing. I was lucky enough to watch one of his chefs make this deep-fried stuffed crab. He made a Chinese roux by frying the flour and then adding oil. Amazing! The dish itself is not super-difficult but you need very fresh crabs to make it sing.

3 tablespoons vegetable oil
1 onion (about 250 g/9 oz), thinly sliced
250 g (9 oz) crab meat
2 tablespoons plain (all-purpose) flour, plus extra
    for dusting
70 ml (2¼ fl oz) milk
4–6 small crab shells
2 eggs, beaten with 3 tablespoons water
60 g (2¼ oz/1 cup) breadcrumbs
Vegetable oil, for deep-frying

Heat 1 tablespoon of the oil in a wok over medium heat, add the onion and fry until softened but not coloured. Remove to a plate. In the same wok, stir-fry the crab meat over medium heat, adding a drop more oil if necessary, until warmed through. Remove to a plate.

Rinse the wok and return to medium–low heat. Add 2 tablespoons of oil and heat until a pinch of flour dropped in begins to bubble, then add the remaining flour and stir over low heat until lightly toasted but not coloured. Add the milk a little at a time, stirring to ensure no lumps form, then return the onion and crab meat to the wok. Mix gently and season with salt and white pepper. Transfer to a bowl and leave to cool.

When ready to serve, lightly dust the inside of each crab shell with flour. Fill with crab mixture and dust again with flour. Brush with the egg wash, then pat breadcrumbs on top. Repeat the crumbing with egg wash and breadcrumbs. (This can be done in advance but the second coating of breadcrumbs must be done just before serving.)

Heat oil for deep-frying in a wok or deep saucepan to 170°C (325°F) and deep-fry the crabs, spooning hot oil over the top, until the breadcrumbs are golden. Serve hot.

vegetables

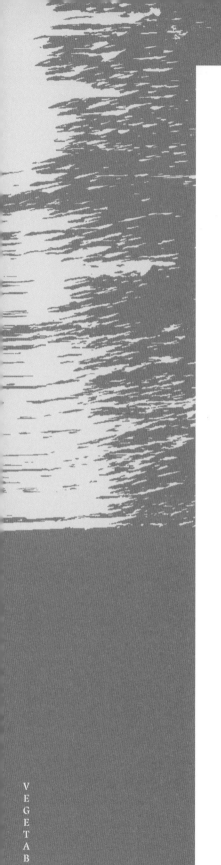

MONG KOK OPEN-AIR MARKET ALONG CANTON ROAD IS A HIVE OF ACTIVITY IN THE EARLY MORNING.

It's already packed with locals shopping for the fresh vegetables and other ingredients that will inspire their daily meals. Trucked in from the New Territories and from farms across the border in Guangdong province, the greens and fruits are a joy to behold.

I'm travelling with my friend Stephanie Alexander, best known for her modern-day bible *The Cook's Companion* and for establishing the Stephanie Alexander Kitchen Foundation, an organisation committed to teaching young Australians in schools the pleasures of growing, cooking and eating good food. What I find exciting about travelling with Stephanie is our shared joy and curiosity for all aspects of food and, in this case, the produce of the land.

As we wander through this neighbourhood market, we marvel at the glistening Asian eggplant, the gorgeous okra in shades of green and purplish red, the bunches of watercress, amaranth with its purple hearts, and the curious-looking kudzu. Along the way, we come across baby bok choy, long beans, garlic chives, Chinese box thorn, taro, two types of edible chrysanthemum, and water chestnuts in their dark coats. Much as we are awed by the incredible range of what are typically known as 'Asian vegetables' in the West, we're also curious about their culinary applications.

Hong Kong is part of the subtropical Pearl River Delta region. Its fertile soil yields fruits such as lychee, jackfruit, papaya, bananas and custard apples alongside figs and strawberries. The land also produces an astonishing range of greens from the brassica family – choy sum and Chinese cabbage being two examples – as well as Ceylon spinach, cucumbers, daikon and lotus root. Although the seasons are not as distinct as in, say, Beijing, Hong Kong has a mild winter so leafy greens are plentiful even in the cooler months. Because of this abundance, Chinese people, especially southerners like me, love eating vegetables. For me, a meal is incomplete without vegetables in one form or another.

The best method of cooking leafy greens such as choy sum, sweet potato leaves, amaranth, water spinach and Chinese broccoli is to stir-fry them in a wok, which seals in the flavours and nutrients. Traditionally, Cantonese cooks use two seasonings – one with garlic and spring onions, and the other with oyster sauce – to lend complexity to vegetables. Lesser-used vegetables such as Ceylon spinach and okra, both of which have a slimy or mucilaginous quality that puts off many people, also benefit from stir-frying.

Not all leafy vegetables are stir-fried. Edible chrysanthemum, also called garland chrysanthemum, much loved for its grassy, aromatic scent and soft leaves, is usually added to hotpots and soups. Watercress and spinach are also marvellous in soups, particularly in summer. This is partly determined by yin and yang, the guiding philosophy of duality in Taoism, which influences Chinese cooking. When the earth is warm in summer it is yang, and to complement this energy it's considered best to eat yin or cooling food. For instance, Chinese cooks use old cucumber, a cooling vegetable, to make a soup with pork, goji berries, dried jujubes and dried scallops. The recipe in this chapter for spinach soup with salted and preserved eggs is a pretty delicious example of yin food.

Root vegetables such as daikon and carrots make regular appearances in pickles, soups and braises. Apparently, the carrot arrived in China via the Middle East in the 14th century in shades of purple and yellow; but it only became popular when the Dutch introduced the orange variety from Taiwan in the 1600s. Old carrots are now used to make tonic soups with herbs such as Solomon's seal, while daikon is turned into the savoury radish 'cake' served as a dim sum item and added to stewed beef dishes.

Mushrooms hold a special place in Chinese gastronomy and have been cultivated for centuries. The most popular is the shiitake mushroom. Prized for their distinctive aroma and meaty flavour, shiitake mushrooms are also known for their medicinal properties. When cooked with ginger, garlic and a splash of Shaoxing, fresh shiitake mushrooms are delicious with rice or on toast. However, many Chinese cooks prefer dried shiitakes because their flavour is more concentrated, especially when they're mixed with king oyster mushrooms and enoki to create a meat-free meal.

Cooking with Chinese vegetables is not about a rigid set of rules and recipes. Instead, it is about being inspired and excited by the sometimes mind-boggling varieties available in fresh, dried and pickled forms. This is especially the case in Hong Kong because of its cosmopolitan nature. Hence I'm thrilled to meet chefs such as Peggy Chan, the lovely owner of Grassroots Pantry. The way she uses vegetables reflects the food trends in contemporary Hong Kong. Ever conscious of issues of the environment and sustainability, her vegetarian menu is not only scrumptious but also eco-friendly. Her recipes in this chapter reflect that approach to using Chinese and Asian ingredients.

In recent times, Hong Kong has also seen an upturn in locally produced organic food and eco-friendly fruit and vegetables. This development is partly due to food-safety concerns over imports from China, and a growing awareness that the city has been too dependent on conventional and organic food flown in from around the world. To meet this growing demand for locally produced greens, organic farms have proliferated in the New Territories and led to the establishment of farmers' markets.

One of the most committed and passionate advocates of organic and sustainable food practices is Janice Leung Hayes. Respected as a food journalist and a firm believer in locally grown produce, Janice founded the Tong Chong Street Market with the Swire group to bring organic farmers and artisan food producers to the public. By far the best farmers' market in town, Tong Chong is an inspiration because it connects farmers to a whole generation of young urban dwellers who are learning the importance of the food cycle. In the process, they're appreciating the connection between the sustainable production of vegetables and their consumption within modern trends towards the use of more fresh and organic foods. This is the joy of cooking greens in Hong Kong.

Lotus root 'meatballs' with roast tomato sauce

Lotus root is much loved in Chinese cooking. It's crunchy with a faint nutty sweet flavour, high in dietary fibre and minerals, and available fresh year round, though also sold frozen. This recipe comes in two parts – the lotus root 'meatballs' and the tomato sauce. The meatballs can be made ahead. This recipe comes from Peggy Chan of Grassroots Pantry, a chef with heart.

250 g (9 oz) lotus root
1 teaspoon ground cumin
½ teaspoon garam masala
½ teaspoon ground coriander
¼ teaspoon chilli powder
3–6 tablespoons chickpea flour
Vegetable oil, for deep-frying
Basil, to garnish

ROAST TOMATO SAUCE
1 kg (2 lb 4 oz) Roma tomatoes
1 teaspoon cumin seeds
2 teaspoons ground cumin
1 teaspoon garam masala
1 tablespoon sunflower oil
3 tablespoons tomato paste
1 large handful basil
2 teaspoons chopped rosemary
2 teaspoons thyme
Pinch of chilli powder
1½ tablespoons coconut sugar

To make the roast tomato sauce, cut a cross at the base of each tomato, place in a large heatproof bowl, pour boiling water over to cover and leave for 2–3 minutes until the skin starts to curl. Drain, peel and halve the tomatoes and remove the seeds. Coarsely chop the tomatoes and blend in a food processor until smooth.

In a large saucepan, fry the cumin seeds, ground cumin and garam masala in oil until fragrant. Add the processed tomatoes, tomato paste, basil, rosemary, thyme and a pinch of salt. Bring to a simmer and cook for 30 minutes or until the mixture is reduced to a thick, chunky sauce-like consistency. Add the chilli powder and coconut sugar. Adjust the seasoning to taste with salt and sugar, and keep warm.

Peel the lotus root, chop into chunks and put in a saucepan. Cover with water, bring to the boil and cook for at least 20 minutes or until cooked through. Drain and allow to cool.

Pulse the lotus root in a food processor until coarsely diced. Add the spices, season with salt and pulse until combined. While mixing, gradually add chickpea flour until the mixture comes together as a dough.

Heat vegetable oil in a deep-fryer or large heavy-based saucepan to 170°C–180°C (325°F–350°F) or until a cube of bread turns golden brown in 10 seconds. Divide the dough into balls the size of ping-pong balls and deep-fry until browned and cooked through. Serve with tomato sauce and garnish with basil.

Vietnamese yellow curry

Serves 4

If there is one restaurant in Hong Kong that believes in sustainability and wellness and still cooks delicious food, Grassroots Pantry is it. Owner-chef Peggy Chan is setting an excellent standard with her plant-based menu. While she is an eco-warrior with years of fine cooking under her belt, she doesn't brandish her beliefs like a zealot. Instead, she lets her outstanding food do the talking. This delicious curry calls for hedgehog mushrooms, but as these are hard to find in Australia I'm using portobello mushrooms instead.

250 g (9 oz) portobello mushrooms
2 tablespoons vegetable oil
½ brown onion, chopped
2 potatoes, peeled and diced
1 large carrot, peeled and diced
200 ml (7 fl oz) coconut milk
1 Asian eggplant (aubergine), diced
1½ tablespoons coconut sugar
500 g (1 lb 2 oz) leafy greens, such as Chinese broccoli,
    spinach or bok choy

MARINADE
10 cm (4 inch) piece ginger, finely grated
2 lemongrass stems, finely chopped
1 tablespoon chilli powder
1½ tablespoons ground turmeric
1 tablespoon tamarind concentrate
2 teaspoons coconut sugar

Combine the marinade ingredients in a bowl, add the mushrooms, cover and leave for 1 hour.

Heat 1 tablespoon vegetable oil in a chargrill pan. Add the mushrooms, reserving the marinade, and grill for 4 minutes or until golden brown. When cool enough to handle, cut into quarters.

Heat the remaining oil in a saucepan. Add the marinade and stir over medium–low heat for 4 minutes until browned and fragrant. Increase the heat to medium, add the onion and stir-fry for 4 minutes. Add the potatoes, carrot and mushrooms and stir gently to combine.

Pour in the coconut milk, bring to the boil and stir, scraping the bottom of the pan to deglaze. Add 100 ml (3½ fl oz) water and return to the boil. Reduce the heat and simmer for 15 minutes, then add the eggplant and simmer for another 15 minutes until the carrot and potatoes are cooked. Add more water if the sauce is reducing too quickly. Stir in the coconut sugar and season with salt and pepper. Add the greens, stir until wilted and serve at once.

V
E
G
E
T
A
B
L
E
S

144

Chiu Chow stir-fried radish

Also known as Four Treasures stir-fry, this is one of the most popular dishes from the Chiu Chow kitchen. This recipe is from my friend Evelyn Yo, whose heritage is Chiu Chow. Evelyn is proud of her ancestry and one of the most knowledgeable cooks I've ever met. This is a fairly simple stir-fry, but you'll need to visit an Asian grocer to pick up some *chye poh*, the Chiu Chow name for sun-dried salted radish. It's an indispensable ingredient in dishes such as *char kway teow*, omelettes and some soups. This recipe also uses a type of compressed or firm tofu – called *tau kwa* in Chiu Chow and Fujian – that's flavoured with Chinese five-spice. It's not common in the West; so, if you can't find it, use regular firm tofu.

200 g (7½ oz) chicken breast, sliced
50 g (1¾ oz) dried shiitake
    mushrooms, soaked in 250 ml
    (9 fl oz/1 cup) hot water for
    30 minutes
125 ml (4 fl oz/½ cup) vegetable oil
100 g (3½ oz) firm tofu, preferably
    flavoured with Chinese five-spice
2 garlic cloves, finely chopped
30 g (1 oz) dried shrimp, rinsed

80 g (2¾ oz) chye poh, sliced
1 long red chilli, seeded and
    thinly sliced

MARINADE
1 tablespoon light soy sauce
1 teaspoon sesame oil
½ teaspoon Shaoxing rice wine
½ teaspoon cornflour (cornstarch)
Pinch of white pepper

Combine the marinade ingredients in a bowl, add the chicken, mix well and set aside for 20 minutes.

Drain the shiitake mushrooms, reserving the soaking liquid. Squeeze out the excess moisture, discard the stems and slice the caps into quarters. Set aside.

Heat 4 tablespoons oil in a wok over medium heat and fry the tofu until slightly crisp. Drain on paper towel, cool, then cut into fine strips. Discard oil.

Wipe out the wok with paper towel, place over medium heat, then add the remaining oil, garlic and dried shrimp and stir-fry for about 3 minutes until fragrant. Transfer the garlic and shrimp with a slotted spoon to paper towel to drain, leaving the oil in the wok.

Increase the heat to medium–high, add the chicken to the wok and stir-fry for 3 minutes. Add the mushrooms and 1–2 tablespoons of the soaking water and stir-fry until the water has evaporated. Add the chye poh and chilli, return the tofu, garlic and dried shrimp to the wok and stir-fry until the mushroom water thickens to a sauce consistency. Check the seasoning and serve.

Stir-fried gai lan

Serves 2-4

When you go to a Chinese restaurant and ask for greens, the waiter often asks whether you'd like them stir-fried with garlic or with oyster sauce, or simply 'clear' fried, meaning finished with stock. Most Chinese diners ask for the green to be cooked with oyster sauce like this stir-fried Chinese broccoli. Belonging to the same family as cauliflower and kale, Chinese broccoli is a joy to eat. It has thick stems and glossy dark-green leaves and is packed with vitamins and minerals. This Cantonese staple is a breeze to cook.

2 tablespoons vegetable oil
400 g (14 oz) gai lan, trimmed and cut into
    8 cm (3 inch) lengths
4 paper-thin slices ginger
1 garlic clove, finely chopped
1 tablespoon Shaoxing rice wine
½ teaspoon sugar
2½ tablespoons chicken stock
1 tablespoon oyster sauce
1 teaspoon light soy sauce
½ teaspoon cornflour (cornstarch), mixed
    with 2 tablespoons water
Pinch of ground white pepper

Bring 1.5 litres (52 fl oz/6 cups) water to the boil in a wok. Add a pinch of salt and 1 tablespoon of the oil, then the Chinese broccoli. Blanch for 1 minute, then tip into a colander and refresh under cold running water. Drain well.

Wipe out the wok with paper towel, return to medium heat and add the remaining oil, ginger and garlic. Stir-fry for 30 seconds until fragrant, return the gai lan to the wok, and stir-fry for a further minute, then add the Shaoxing rice wine, sugar, stock, oyster sauce and soy sauce. Bring to a simmer and, when the sauce has slightly reduced, stir in the cornflour mixture and simmer to thicken further. Adjust the seasoning with salt and white pepper and serve hot.

Note *Chinese broccoli is sold young and fresh in Hong Kong. In the West it tends to be larger and more fibrous with thicker stems, which need to be peeled before cooking.*

Stir-fried bitter melon with egg

Serves 2

As the name suggests, bitter melon is astringent and it can be an acquired taste. I was seduced by this much-maligned fruit as a kid when my mother cooked a variety called 'white jade' in Chinese. It tastes somewhat sweet with a subtle bitter edge, and my mother cooked it with lots of salted black beans and chillies. It's also wonderful stuffed with meat or shaved thinly in a salad. If you haven't eaten bitter melon before, select one with a paler colour for this home-style dish; zucchini (courgette) is a great substitute. This dish is also delicious with chopped boiled salted egg tossed through.

1 x 350 g (12 oz) bitter melon
1 teaspoon dried shrimp, soaked in hot water
    for 20 mintues
1 tablespoon vegetable oil
1 garlic clove, finely chopped
2 red Asian shallots, finely chopped
1 teaspoon finely chopped ginger
125 ml (4 fl oz/½ cup) chicken stock
1 tablespoon light soy sauce
Pinch of sugar
1 egg, mixed with 1 tablespoon water

Wash the bitter melon and trim off the stem. Slice the melon in half lengthways and scoop out the pith and seeds. Thinly slice the melon crossways into 1 cm (½ inch) rounds.

Drain and chop the shrimp. Place a wok over medium–high heat. As soon as it starts to smoke, add the vegetable oil, garlic, shallots and ginger. Fry until fragrant, then add the shrimp. Stir-fry for 30 seconds, then add the bitter melon. Continue to stir-fry until the melon slices are lightly browned.

Add the chicken stock, soy sauce and sugar, bring to the boil and cook until the liquid has reduced by half. Taste and adjust the seasoning with salt and pepper. Stir in the egg until just scrambled, then serve at once.

Braised wild mushrooms

Serves 4-6

Chinese people are not only crazy about mushrooms, but they also value them for their medicinal properties. Braised mushrooms, especially shiitake, are a traditional favourite and often served as part of Chinese New Year celebrations. I don't remember when or where I first ate this dish – probably at a *poon choi* (see Note) feast with friends in a walled village out in the New Territories – but it's delicious. What's great about this dish is that you can use virtually any mushrooms such as monkey heads, morels and chanterelles. For this recipe, I've chosen mushrooms that are readily available from your Asian supermarket. This dish is delicious teamed with chicken and duck.

100 g (3½ oz) dried shiitake mushrooms, soaked
    in warm water for 30 minutes
200 g (7 oz) king oyster mushrooms
100 g (3½ oz) enoki mushrooms
2 tablespoons vegetable oil
2 spring onions (scallions), white part only,
    finely chopped
2 tablespoons finely chopped ginger
2 garlic cloves, finely chopped
2 tablespoons Shaoxing rice wine
1 tablespoon oyster sauce
1 teaspoon dark soy sauce
2 tablespoons light soy sauce
500 ml (17 fl oz/2 cups) chicken stock
Pinch of sugar, or to taste
2 teaspoons cornflour (cornstarch), mixed
    with 2 tablespoons water
1 teaspoon sesame oil
Chopped coriander, to garnish

Squeeze the excess water from the shiitake mushrooms and cut off the stems. Cut into quarters, or halve if they're small. Slice the king oyster mushrooms in half and cut each half into bite-sized pieces. Trim off the woody ends of the enoki mushrooms and separate into clusters.

Heat the oil in a wok over medium–high heat. Add the spring onions, ginger and garlic and stir-fry until fragrant. Add the shiitake mushrooms and stir-fry for 1 minute, then add the king oyster mushrooms and stir-fry for another minute. Add the Shaoxing rice wine, oyster sauce, soy sauces, chicken stock and sugar and bring to the boil. Reduce the heat to medium–low, cover the wok with a lid and cook for 20–30 minutes to let the mushrooms absorb the flavours. If the stock reduces too quickly, add extra to keep enough for the sauce. Season with salt and pepper and then add the enoki. Stir in the cornflour mixture and stir until thickened, then add the sesame oil.

Serve garnished with chopped coriander.

Note

Poon choi *is unique to Hong Kong, and the New Territories in particular. It's a communal dish comprising layers of ingredients such as taro, daikon, pig skin, roast duck, chicken and prawns, usually served during Chinese New Year. Legend has it that a Song emperor fleeing the Mongols some 700 years ago was served this dish. As the villagers had few containers, the food was layered meticulously in a wooden wash basin. Thus was born the* first poon choi.

HONG KONG FOOD CITY

Fish-fragrant eggplant

Probably as famous as ma po doufu, fish-fragrant eggplant from Sichuan is another classic. There's no fish in this dish – the name refers to the hot, sweet, sour and spicy flavours that are used in Sichuan-style seafood dishes. The eggplant is typically served buttery soft, although recently some Sichuan restaurants have been coating it with a light dusting of cornflour before deep-frying and serving it crisp and crunchy.

1 teaspoon caster (superfine) sugar, or to taste
2 tablespoons Chinkiang vinegar
100 ml (3½ fl oz) chicken stock
Vegetable oil, for deep-frying
2 eggplants (aubergines), cut into finger-sized strips
4 spring onions (scallions), white part only,
    finely chopped
1 tablespoon finely chopped ginger
4 cloves garlic, finely chopped
1–2 tablespoons doubanjiang (Sichuan chilli
    bean paste)
2 tablespoons Shaoxing rice wine
1 tablespoon potato flour, mixed with
    2 tablespoons water
Thinly sliced spring onion (scallions), to garnish

Mix the sugar, Chinkiang vinegar and chicken stock in a bowl and set aside.

Heat oil for deep-frying in a wok over medium–high heat to 180°C (350°F) or until it begins to smoke. Add the eggplant in batches and deep-fry for 3–4 minutes per batch until just golden on the outside and soft inside. Lift out with a slotted spoon onto paper towel to drain.

Carefully pour the oil into a heatproof container (reserve for another use). Wipe out the wok with paper towel, add 2 tablespoons of the reserved oil and place over medium heat. Add the spring onions, ginger and garlic and stir-fry for 30 seconds until fragrant, then add the doubanjiang and stir-fry until fragrant; if the wok gets too hot, reduce the heat or lift it off the stove briefly.

Return the eggplant to the wok, deglaze the pan with Shaoxing rice wine, then add the vinegar–chicken stock mixture. Reduce the heat and simmer until the stock is reduced slightly.

Add the potato flour mixture and stir gently until the sauce thickens. Transfer to a serving platter, scatter with spring onions and serve.

Sichuan dry-fried green beans

Serves 2-4

This popular dish from Sichuan province pops up frequently in restaurants such as the legendary Da Ping Huo in Central, and Sijie Sichuan in Wan Chai. Dry-fried green beans is an addictive dish if you love hot and numbing flavours. Traditionally the beans are fried in very little oil until they blister and wrinkle and take on a smoky flavour. Nowadays many cooks deep-fry the beans to speed up the process. In most homes, minced pork is used, but minced beef and chicken work beautifully, too. This is an easy dish to make and, from experience, it's marvellous with a bowl of congee.

Vegetable oil, for deep-frying
300 g (10½ oz) green beans, trimmed
2 garlic cloves, finely chopped
1 teaspoon finely chopped ginger
2 spring onions (scallions), white part only,
　　finely chopped
1 teaspoon Sichuan peppercorns, crushed
4–5 dried chillies, trimmed
50 g (1¾ oz) minced (ground) pork
2 tablespoons chopped ya cai or any pickled Chinese
　　vegetable (see Note)
1 tablespoon Shaoxing rice wine
1 teaspoon light soy sauce

Heat oil for deep-frying in a wok to 170°C (325°F) or until a cube of bread turns golden brown in 20 seconds. Add the green beans and deep-fry for 2 minutes until they blister. Remove with a slotted spoon and drain well. Carefully pour the hot oil into a heatproof container (reserve for another use), leaving 2 tablespoons in the wok.

Add the garlic, ginger, spring onions, Sichuan peppercorns and chillies to the wok and stir-fry over medium heat until fragrant.

Add the pork and ya cai and stir-fry for 3–4 minutes over medium heat. Splash in the rice wine and light soy sauce and stir a few times. Return the green beans to the wok and continue to stir-fry for 1–2 minutes until nicely coated. Serve immediately with steamed rice.

Note *Ya cai is a pickled Chinese vegetable from Yibin province in Sichuan. Use any leafy pickled Chinese vegetable from your Asian grocer if it's not available.*

rice and noodles

THE DAY IS COLD FROM THE INCESSANT RAIN AND A BITTER WIND BLOWS FROM THE NORTH. FACES LOOK GRIM AND RESIGNED AS WINTER SETS IN.

But as the crowds walk down the main street of Shau Kei Wan, a town on the north-eastern side of Hong Kong Island, their faces light up as they approach a brightly lit hole in the wall. I'm in unfamiliar territory and I'm hungry, so I follow the crowd. The front window reveals a small kitchen and several plastic tubs piled high with slices of raw fish and beef, minced pork, liver, chopped spring onions. Also on display is a huge cauldron of rice porridge. Ah! *Jook!* I promptly order a bowl of the soothing, silky stuff with sliced fish and chopped ginger. Suddenly the world seems bright again.

Jook is the local vernacular for rice porridge. Like the much-loved Jewish chicken soup, it's the Chinese panacea for everything bad. Also called congee, it's arguably the most-loved rice dish in Hong Kong and southern China. It's easy to make and, like steamed rice, it's bland but springs to life when given a splash of umami-rich soy sauce and other life-affirming ingredients.

Rice is indispensable in Chinese gastronomy. Without it, and soy beans, the Chinese food world would not be what it is today. The starchy grain of the grass family, rice comes in several varieties. In China, medium- and short-grained varieties are grown, both glutinous and non-glutinous. The fluffy white rice commonly served in restaurants is the non-glutinous type.

Rice is traditionally cooked using the absorption method. First rinse the grains until the water runs clear, then put the rice in a pan and cover it with water to reach the first joint of your middle finger. Bring to the boil and, depending on how much rice is in the pan, it should take 10–12 minutes for most of the water to be absorbed and vent holes to appear on the surface. Cover the pan and leave it to cook on the lowest heat for another 10–15 minutes. This cooked rice will be the perfect canvas for stir-fried and steamed dishes. If you're a frequent rice eater, it pays to invest in an electric rice cooker.

I tend to err on the generous side when cooking rice and use any leftover to make fried rice. Like risotto, fried rice has many friends – just about any ingredient will make this dish sing. The most famous is from Yangzhou (see page 172), a city in China's Jiangsu province. Made with char siu, prawns, peas and spring onions, this celebrated dish frequently appears at Chinese weddings and banquets. My favourite is Macanese fried rice (page 162), a delicious hybrid of Chinese and Portuguese influences from Macau. This region is best known as the Vegas of China, but its food also makes it worthy of a detour.

Another famous rice dish is made in a claypot with a glazed interior. Called *bo zai* in Cantonese, these pots are similar to the Spanish *cazuela*. This old-school number is usually made with lap cheong and waxed pork, which permeate the rice as they cook to create a most distinctive flavour, along with the coveted crusty layer that forms on the base (page 178). In Hong Kong, claypot aficionados flock to the no-nonsense Kwan Kee in Sai Ying Pun and Ser Wong Fun in Central, also famed for its snake dishes.

Also called 'sticky rice', glutinous rice is gluten free – its misleading name refers simply to the sticky nature of this grain. It's served as a dim sum item steamed in lotus leaf (see page 190) and ground to make sweet snacks. Black and white glutinous rice is also used to make wine and some vinegars.

Rice, along with wheat, mung beans, buckwheat and sweet potatoes, is also made into noodles. Of these, rice and wheat noodles are the most popular and some restaurants offer both.

Noodles are deeply rooted in Hong Kong's culinary consciousness and are the source of much debate, with locals warring over matters of shape and texture. From the prosaic 'cart noodles', so named because they were once served from pushcarts when vendors roamed the streets, to the ultimate in noodle luxury, such as noodles topped with lobster, the story of noodles spans the full culinary spectrum.

Often eaten at lunchtime or when a quick fix is needed, noodles are enjoyed in several forms. Some are stir-fried, while others are added to soups. But in Hong Kong's noodle universe, wonton noodles are the ultimate comfort food. This is a dish that will elicit sighs of nostalgia, hunger, warmth and home. Wonton noodles might look simple to prepare but it's the quality of three elements that makes the dish really shine: a superb broth made with pork bones and grilled dried plaice; eggy, springy noodles; and wontons filled with nuggets of fresh prawn and pork. After sampling countless versions of wonton noodles, I consider Mak's Noodles in Central and Ho Hung Kee in Causeway Bay still the best. Be prepared to queue for their ethereal wontons. The servings at these institutions tend to be small, but there's magic in the bowl.

Stir-fried beef noodles is another of Hong Kong's much-loved dishes. Properly made, it's intensely satisfying and tasty. This is typically served in *cha chaan tengs* and *dai pai dongs* and one of the best I've had was at Tasty Congee and Noodle Wonton Shop in Central. Made with fresh wide rice noodles, its unmistakable wok fragrance is the key to the success of this dish.

Art meets noodle-making when it comes to beautiful bamboo noodles, made by a traditional method that is sadly dying out. Seeing the noodle master kneading the dough with a bamboo pole is like watching a ballet dancer in motion – he rides the pole to bounce it in a rhythmic action that develops the gluten and eventually turns it into fine strands of noodles. Usually eaten with dried shrimp roe and a bowl of clear broth, these handmade noodles are served at Kwan Kee Bamboo Noodle in Cheung Sha Wan.

Rice and noodles, staples in the Hong Kong food world, nourish as much as they inspire. If you happen to be in Wan Chai, check out Kang Kee Noodles, a tiny flour-covered shop that's virtually an institution. Its marvellous selection of fresh and dried noodles is simply a joy to behold.

While we might not have the luxury of such a shop in the West, virtually all types of rice and noodles are readily available in Chinese grocery stores. The recipes in this chapter are wonderfully approachable: please try.

Macanese fried rice with cod

Serves 2

Just under an hour by ferry from Hong Kong is Macau, which was colonised by the Portuguese in 1557. By the time it was returned to China in 1999, a lovely blend of Portuguese and Cantonese cuisines with some influence from Goa and Mozambique had evolved into a Macanese cuisine. This exceptionally tasty dish of fried rice is a fine example of this unique blend. It features salt cod – *baccalà*, or *bacalhau* in Portuguese – and is a cinch to make. Some cooks and restaurants add olives – don't be surprised to find this hybrid dish made with all sorts of different goodies. If you visit Macau, check out António restaurant and Albergue 1601 for Portuguese and Macanese food.

3 tablespoons extra virgin olive oil, plus extra to serve
1 egg, beaten
1 red Asian shallot, finely chopped
120 g (4¼ oz) shop-bought, soaked and drained salt
   cod, cut into small cubes
500 g (1 lb 2 oz) cooked long-grain rice, preferably
   refrigerated overnight
30 g (1 oz) green capsicums (peppers), finely diced
1 spring onion (scallion), finely chopped
1 small tomato, sliced

Put the olive oil in a wok over medium–high heat. Pour in the egg and tilt the wok to form a thin omelette. Move the omelette to the side and add the shallot. Stir-fry for 30 seconds, then add the baccalà, adding more oil if needed.

Stir-fry for 1–2 minutes, then add the rice and stir-fry until hot. Add the capsicum and spring onion, season with salt and white pepper and stir-fry for another minute. Drizzle some extra oil over the rice and serve with sliced tomato.

Wonton noodle soup

If there's one dish to eat in Hong Kong, it's wonton noodle soup. As comforting as a bowl of pho, this dish has three elements: a soup, al dente egg noodles and bouncy wontons. It's a simple dish but, like all things simple, it requires top ingredients to make it shine. For starters, the soup must be clear and flavoursome; it's traditionally made with a combination of pork bones, chicken carcasses and dried shrimp, although institutions such as Mak's Noodles and Ho Hung Kee add roasted dried flounder, too. Should you wish to go the extra mile to make the broth similar to those in Hong Kong, you can find dried flounder in Asian supermarkets; simply toast it before adding it to the soup. My recipe for the wonton filling uses prawns and pork, but you can make it all pork or all prawns if you like. Wonton, by the way, means 'swallowing clouds'.

3 litres (105 fl oz/12 cups)
   chicken stock
1 tablespoon dried shrimp, rinsed
50 g (1¾ oz) piece dried flounder
   (optional)
2 thin slices ginger
1 tablespoon Shaoxing rice wine
1 tablespoon light soy sauce
700 g (1 lb 9 oz) fresh thin
   egg noodles
2 spring onions (scallions),
   thinly sliced
Soy sauce and red rice vinegar,
   to serve

PORK AND PRAWN WONTONS
300 g (10½ oz) peeled uncooked
   prawns, coarsely chopped
100 g (3½ oz) minced (ground) pork
2 dried wood ear mushrooms,
   finely chopped
1 small egg, beaten
½ teaspoon sugar
½ teaspoon sesame oil
1 tablespoon light soy sauce
20–25 square wonton wrappers

For the wontons, combine the prawns, pork, mushrooms, egg, sugar, sesame oil and soy sauce in a bowl and season with salt and white pepper. Mix well.

Fill a small bowl with water. Working with one wonton wrapper at a time, place a teaspoonful of filling in the centre of the wrapper, dip your finger in the water and run it around the edges of the wrapper. Fold over to form a triangle, then dab one of the lower corners with water, fold over to the other lower corner and pinch with your thumb and index finger to seal. Cover the filled wontons with a tea towel while you make the soup. Makes 20–25 wontons.

To make the soup, put the chicken stock, dried shrimp, dried flounder, ginger and Shaoxing in a saucepan and bring to the boil. Simmer for 5–10 minutes. Add the light soy sauce and season to taste. Cover and keep warm.

Cook the noodles for 2–4 minutes in boiling salted water until tender. Drain and divide among warm bowls.

Cook the wontons in batches in boiling salted water, for 2–3 minutes each batch, until they rise to the surface. Remove with a slotted spoon and add to the bowls. Bring the soup back to the boil and pour into the bowls. Scatter with spring onions and serve with soy sauce and red rice vinegar.

Stir-fried beef hor fun noodles

Serves 2

Hor fun is the Cantonese name for rice stick noodles. Looking a bit like white fettuccine, these flat noodles are sold both fresh and dried. A favourite with locals and visitors alike, this fast one-dish meal is noted for its *wok hei* – that elusive but distinctive breath of the wok created when food is cooked quickly in a very hot wok. The recipe is super-easy – the beef is marinated and fried, then the noodles are fried separately with onion and spring onions, and finally the beef and bean shoots are added. It's given a good blast of heat and voilà – the dish is ready in minutes. If your wok is small, cook the recipe in two batches to achieve the wok fragrance.

150–200 g (5½–7 oz) beef fillet or rump,
    cut into very thinly slices
3 tablespoons vegetable oil
300 g (10½ oz) fresh hor fun noodles
3 spring onions (scallions), cut into short lengths
1 small brown onion, thinly sliced
1 tablespoon oyster sauce
1 tablespoon light soy sauce
1 teaspoon dark soy sauce
1 large handful bean sprouts, trimmed
Sliced red chillies, mixed with light soy sauce, to serve

MARINADE
1 tablespoon light soy sauce
2 teaspoons cornflour (cornstarch)
2 teaspoons ginger juice, squeezed from 4 tablespoons
    grated ginger
1 teaspoon bicarbonate of soda (baking soda)

Mix the marinade ingredients in a bowl, season with salt and pepper and add the beef. Mix well and leave to marinate for 10–15 minutes.

Heat 1 tablespoon oil in a wok over high heat. Add the beef and stir-fry for 1 minute until partially cooked and browned. Transfer to a plate.

Wipe out the wok with paper towel and return to the heat. When hot and slightly smoky, add 2 tablespoons oil. When the oil is shimmering, add the noodles and toss for 2–3 minutes, taking care not to break up the noodles. Add the spring onions and onion, toss again for 20 seconds, then add the oyster sauce and soy sauces. Stir well.

Return the beef to the wok, add the bean sprouts and season with salt and pepper. Stir-fry for another minute and serve immediately with sliced red chillies in light soy sauce on the side.

Crab with glass noodles

Glass noodles have multiple names in English, including cellophane, mung bean, bean thread and crystal noodles. They're usually made of mung bean flour or mung bean starch, although some are made of yams or sweet potatoes. On their own, these slippery noodles don't have much taste, but they soak up the flavours of other ingredients. My favourite brand is Longkou. Eating whole crabs is pretty hands-on and somewhat messy, but this luxurious seafood is fun to share at home with family and friends. I've used blue swimmer crabs for this recipe, but any variety of crab will work well. This dish is traditionally served in a claypot.

1.2 kg (2 lb 12 oz) fresh crab
100 g (3½ oz) glass noodles
1 tablespoon dried shrimp, rinsed
Seasoned plain (all-purpose) flour,
    for dusting
4 tablespoons vegetable oil
3 garlic cloves, finely chopped
2 large red Asian shallots,
    thinly sliced
3 tablespoons finely chopped ginger
2 spring onions (scallions), julienned

SAUCE
2 tablespoons light soy sauce
2 tablespoons oyster sauce
3 tablespoons mild rice wine
2 teaspoons sesame oil
1 teaspoon caster (superfine) sugar
3 tablespoons chopped coriander
500 ml (17 fl oz/2 cups) chicken
    stock

If you're using live crab, kill it humanely by placing it in the freezer for a couple of hours to put it to sleep, then place it on its back, lift off the top shell or carapace and pierce it with a sharp knife. Discard the carapace, or keep it for presentation. Remove the V-shaped flap and gills, discard the bony bits at the head and rinse off any brown mustard. Cut the body into quarters and crack the claws with the back of a cleaver or with a mallet. Set aside.

Soak the glass noodles in warm water for 10 minutes, then drain well. Cut into manageable sections and set aside. Cover the rinsed shrimps with warm water to soak until softened (about 10 minutes). Drain and chop finely.

Combine the sauce ingredients in a small bowl and set aside

When ready to cook, dust the crab lightly with flour. Heat half the oil in a wok over medium–high heat, add the crab and stir-fry for 4–5 minutes until starting to turn orange, then transfer to a plate.

Add the remaining oil to the hot wok and sprinkle in the chopped shrimp, garlic, shallots and ginger. Stir-fry for 2 minutes or until golden and fragrant. Add the sauce ingredients and crab, bring to the boil, then reduce the heat and simmer for 4–5 minutes until the crab is almost cooked through and sauce is slightly thickened. Add the noodles and toss well.

As soon as the noodles turn transparent, dish out into a heated claypot, sprinkle with spring onions and serve.

Yangzhou fried rice

Serves 2-4

In Hong Kong, the Cantonese call this classic *yeung chow* fried rice. Often served to mark the end of a banquet and also a great comfort food that can be whipped up in minutes, this fried rice is my go-to dish when friends drop by unexpectedly. It's named after Yangzhou, a famous city in Jiangsu province. Cold cooked rice is ideal for this dish, preferably after being refrigerated overnight. Ideally, fried rice should have *wok hei*, the smoky fragrance that's the hallmark of great Chinese cooking, created by cooking food quickly in a very hot wok. Heat is of vital importance for the best fried rice, so cook it in two batches if your wok is small.

600 g (1 lb 5 oz) cooked jasmine rice
5 tablespoons vegetable oil
100 g (3½ oz) peeled uncooked prawns, deveined
    and diced
2 free-range eggs, beaten
100 g (3½ oz) barbecued pork (char siu) or lap cheong
    sausage, diced
50 g (1¾ oz) peas, blanched
2 small spring onions (scallions), sliced into fine rings
1 teaspoon sesame oil
1 tablespoon light soy sauce

Separate the cooked rice grains with a fork as much as possible. Set aside.

Heat a wok over high heat until just smoking. Add 1 tablespoon oil and, when hot, add the prawns and stir-fry until just cooked. Transfer to a plate.

Add 2 tablespoons oil to the wok and swirl to coat. Add the eggs and stir-fry until just set, then transfer to a plate.

Add the remaining oil and, when very hot, add the char siu and rice and stir-fry for 2–3 minutes, moving everything around to stop it sticking. Use a ladle or wok scoop to break up any lumps until the grains are well separated.

Add the peas and return the prawns and eggs to the wok, and stir-fry until the rice is very hot and fragrant. Add the spring onions, sesame oil and soy sauce and stir-fry for another 30 seconds or until everything is coated and coloured. By now the rice grains should pop or jump. Taste and adjust the seasoning with salt and freshly ground white pepper. Serve at once.

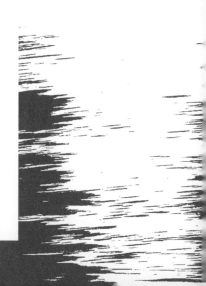

Congee with fish and ginger

Serves 4

Congee or rice porridge (*jook* in Cantonese) is a wonderful food found just about everywhere in Hong Kong, mainland China and throughout South-east Asia. Soothing and comfortable and ever so gentle on the tummy, it's sold at stalls from dawn until dusk. Some congee lovers like it runny, while others, like me, prefer it creamy and silky. This takes a little longer to allow the grains to 'burst' or break down. Congee is typically served with a host of condiments such as salted duck eggs, pickles, fermented bean curd, and roasted peanuts – it's entirely up to individual preference. My mother loved adding sweet potato to her congee and at other times sliced fish and ginger. This is her recipe but by all means experiment. It's a breeze to make.

150 g (5½ oz) medium-grain rice
2.5 litres (87 fl oz/10 cups) chicken stock or water
1 tablespoon vegetable oil
2 tablespoons thinly sliced ginger
250 g (9 oz) white-fleshed fish such as grouper
    or snapper, thinly sliced
1 tablespoon light soy sauce
1 teaspoon sesame oil
1 tablespoon Shaoxing rice wine
½ teaspoon ground white pepper
2 spring onions (scallions), finely chopped

GARNISHES
1 small handful chopped coriander
2 tablespoons fried shallots
2 tablespoons roasted peanuts
2 tablespoons pickled greens

Rinse and drain the rice, place in a large saucepan with the chicken stock or water and bring to the boil. Reduce the heat to a low simmer, cover partially and simmer gently for about 1½ hours until thick and creamy, stirring occasionally to prevent it sticking. If it's too thick, add a little water or stock, and if it's too runny, simmer it a little longer. Mix in the vegetable oil, shredded ginger and salt to taste.

While the congee is simmering, marinate the fish slices with light soy sauce, sesame oil, Shaoxing rice wine and pepper.

Once the congee is cooked, add the fish to the pan, put the lid on and simmer for 3–5 minutes. Serve in bowls, topped with spring onions and other garnishes.

Home-style stir-fried rice vermicelli with pork and greens

Serves 2

This is one of the instant dishes I cook for my family whenever I'm in Hong Kong. It's pretty straightforward and can be whipped up in a matter of minutes. It's also perfect for people with gluten intolerance – just use tamari in place of the soy sauce and skip the oyster sauce unless, of course, it's made without flour. Chicken or seafood work well in place of the pork, or use mushrooms for a meat-free dish.

150 g (5½ oz) lean pork, thinly sliced
200 g (7 oz) dried rice vermicelli, soaked briefly
    in hot water
2–3 tablespoons vegetable oil
2 spring onions (scallions), cut into short lengths
2 garlic cloves, finely chopped
1 tablespoon oyster sauce
1 teaspoon light soy sauce
1 teaspoon dark soy sauce
125 ml (4 fl oz/½ cup) chicken stock
120 g (4¼ oz) choy sum, chopped
½ teaspoon sesame oil
Pickled chillies, to serve

MARINADE
1 tablespoon Shaoxing rice wine
1 teaspoon light soy sauce
1 teaspoon cornflour (cornstarch)

Mix together the marinade ingredients, salt, white pepper and 1 teaspoon water in a bowl. Add the pork, toss well and leave to marinate for 10 minutes.

When you're ready to cook, drain the vermicelli well.

Heat the oil in a wok until smoking, add the spring onions and garlic and stir-fry for 30 seconds, then add the pork and toss for another 30 seconds. Add the noodles and toss for 2 minutes, then add the oyster sauce, light and dark soy sauces and half the chicken stock. Stir-fry for another 30 seconds, then add the remaining stock. Reduce the heat to medium and keep tossing for another 2 minutes, taking care not to break up the noodles.

Add the choy sum and cook until just wilted. Add the sesame oil, toss to combine and serve with pickled chillies.

Cantonese claypot rice

Serves 2

This one-pot meal is one of my favourite dishes when the weather turns cold. Traditionally, chicken, lap cheong sausage and shiitake mushrooms are the usual suspects for flavouring the rice, but I've also had this with goose-liver sausage, frogs' legs and salted fish. The best claypot rice I've eaten was at the very old-school Kwan Kee in the Western District of Hong Kong Island. This recipe is Cantonese in origin, but there are several versions of this popular dish. Should you use a Chinese claypot, a good trick is to drizzle ½ tablespoon of oil around the side of the pot after the rice is just cooked so it forms a firmer crust.

150 g (5 oz) boneless chicken thighs, diced
3 dried shiitake mushrooms, soaked in hot water until softened, squeezed dry
2 tablespoons vegetable oil
20 g (¾ oz) salted fish (see Note), diced
1 teaspoon finely chopped garlic
1 tablespoon julienned ginger
1 lap cheong sausage, thinly sliced
200 g (7 oz/1 cup) long-grain rice, rinsed and drained well
310 ml (10¾ fl oz/1¼ cups) chicken stock or water

2 baby bok choy, trimmed and blanched
Chopped coriander (cilantro), to garnish

MARINADE
1 tablespoon light soy sauce
1 tablespoon oyster sauce
1 tablespoon ginger juice, squeezed from grated fresh ginger
½ teaspoon sugar
½ teaspoon dark soy sauce
½ teaspoon Chinese five-spice
1 tablespoon Shaoxing rice wine
1 teaspoon sesame oil

Combine the marinade ingredients in a bowl, add the chicken, toss to coat well and set aside for 30 minutes. Discard the stems from the mushrooms and slice the caps into quarters.

Heat the oil in a claypot over medium heat. Add the salted fish, fry until golden and then transfer to a plate. Add the garlic, ginger, lap cheong and shiitake mushrooms to the pot and stir-fry for 15 seconds. Add the chicken and stir-fry until partially cooked. Remove everything from the pot and mix with the salted fish.

Add the rice to the pot and stir well to coat with the oil, then add the stock or water and bring to the boil. Cover the pot with a lid and simmer for 10 minutes. Return the chicken and salted fish mixture to the pot, cover and cook until all the liquid has been absorbed and the rice is cooked through.

Turn off the heat, add the bok choy, cover and leave for 3 minutes. Sprinkle with coriander and serve.

Note *Salted fish comes in different varieties, such as mergui and snapper; use whatever is available from your Asian grocer.*

Wontons with red chilli oil

Serves 4-6

I adore Cantonese wontons in soups, but every once in a while I get a craving for Sichuan's spicy wontons. Called *hong you chao shou* in Mandarin, these delicious dumplings are pretty common in Sichuan province but less so in Hong Kong. They're a cinch to make and the accompanying hot sauce with toasty chilli takes these morsels to another level.

360 g (12¾ oz) packet square wonton wrappers
2 spring onions (scallions), thinly sliced

FILLING
300 g (10½ oz) minced (ground) pork with
    30% fat content
2 tablespoons finely chopped ginger
1 tablespoon light soy sauce
½ teaspoon sugar
2 teaspoons Shaoxing rice wine
1 egg, beaten
3 tablespoons chicken stock

RED CHILLI OIL
1 tablespoon white sesame seeds, roasted
2 garlic cloves, finely chopped
1 tablespoon finely chopped ginger
3 tablespoons light soy sauce
1 teaspoon Sichuan peppercorns
185 ml (6 fl oz/¾ cup) chilli oil with sediment
    (see page 244)
1 tablespoon sesame oil
Pinch of sugar, or to taste

To make the filling, put all the ingredients except the chicken stock in a bowl and mix well. Add the stock a tablespoon at a time, stirring in a circular motion until incorporated before adding the next spoonful.

Fill a small bowl with water. Working with one wonton wrapper at a time, place a teaspoonful of pork filling in the centre of the wrapper. Dip your finger in the water and run it around the edges of the wrapper. Fold over to form a triangle, then dab one of the lower corners with water and fold over to the other lower corner and pinch with your thumb and index finger to seal. Repeat until all the filling is used. Makes 30–40 wontons.

Mix together all the red chilli oil ingredients in a bowl.

Bring a large saucepan of water to the boil and cook the wontons in batches until they float to the surface. Remove with a slotted spoon. Divide the wontons among serving bowls, drizzle with chilli oil and garnish with spring onions.

Tomato noodles

Serves 4

This dish is certainly not particularly highbrow, but if you're after a slice of Hong Kong's food history and culture, then make a pilgrimage to Sing Heung Yuen to try it. One of the last remaining *dai pai dong* in Central, this food stall is like a time capsule. Be prepared to sit on rickety chairs and dine alfresco among the crowds of locals and visitors who come for the nostalgic and delicious food. On the menu are 'Soy Sauce Western' offerings, such as toasted dinner rolls with marmalade, peanut butter or condensed milk, along with the likes of macaroni or instant noodles with Spam, sausage and braised beef in a rich tomato broth. I've been addicted to their tomato broth ever since I first ate there. This is my version. If you're famished, you can whip this up in 10 to 15 minutes.

200 g (7 oz) dried udon noodles or
    4 packets instant noodles
2 tablespoons vegetable oil
2 garlic cloves, finely chopped
2 red Asian shallots, finely chopped
2 teaspoons finely chopped ginger
200 g (7 oz) tomatoes, seeded and chopped
800 g (1 lb 12 oz) canned chopped tomatoes
1 litre (35 fl oz/4 cups) chicken stock
1 tablespoon light soy sauce
Sugar, to taste
1 teaspoon sesame oil
Chopped spring onions (scallions), to garnish

Bring a large saucepan of water to the boil and cook the noodles according to the instructions on the packet. Drain and transfer to a bowl. Toss with a soupçon of oil to keep the noodles from sticking. Keep warm.

Meanwhile, heat a large saucepan or wok over medium heat and add the oil. When hot, add the garlic, shallots and ginger and stir-fry until aromatic. Add the fresh tomatoes and stir briefly, then add the canned tomatoes and stock. Increase the heat to high and cook until the tomatoes have softened. Add the soy sauce and sugar to taste. Drizzle with sesame oil and check the seasoning.

Divide the noodles among serving bowls and ladle in the tomato broth. Garnish with spring onions and serve.

dim sum

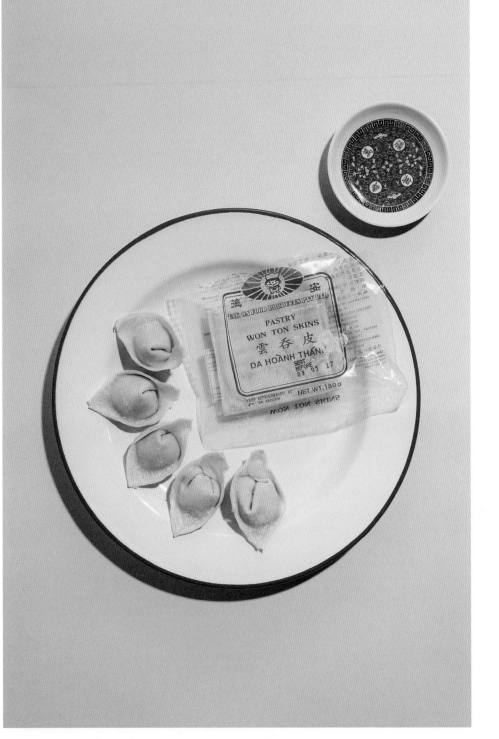

EVEN BEFORE THE PLANE TOUCHES DOWN AT HONG KONG'S CHEK LAP KOK AIRPORT, MY STOMACH IS GROWLING FOR DIM SUM.

Yes, it's my weakness and my obsession. I reckon anyone who loves dim sum (meaning 'touch your heart') knows Hong Kong is the city for the best.

Take cult-status Tim Ho Wan, for instance. The quality of the food at this hole-in-the-wall joint was so impressive that the Michelin judges awarded it a star, making it the cheapest starred dining spot in the world. Started by Mak Kwai Pui, a former chef of three-Michelin-starred Lung King Heen restaurant, it was an instant hit.

With so many good dim sum places around town, deciding which to go to is pretty hard. I've been to places such as the Metropole and Maxim's City Hall where dim sum treats are served from traditional trolleys. I've also been to old-school teahouses such as Luk Yu where waitresses parade the dim sum on trays slung on their shoulders.

I've also lunched at Lung King Heen where biting into a tiny morsel of dim sum has you in raptures. At raucous places such as Lin Heung it's customary to scald your chopsticks and bowl in hot tea while customers hover behind you waiting for you to eat up quickly and leave.

Dim sum started long ago with the tea-drinking tradition. To accompany the tea, tiny morsels were offered (much like tapas with wine in Spanish taverns). You often hear the Cantonese term *yum cha* ('drink tea') when you are invited to a lunch of dim sum. Hence the name yum cha for the meal when dim sum are served, typically from dawn to lunchtime, although some restaurants now serve dim sum in the evenings.

Since tea is the reason for eating dim sum, you're often asked by the waiter what tea is your preference. Most Chinese diners ask for *po lei* or *pu er*, a fermented tea known for its beneficial qualities. But, when in doubt, ask what is being offered and then decide.

There are virtually hundreds of dim sum and any self-respecting restaurant has to offer at least 50 varieties. Some places have a paper menu where you tick your selection, so it pays to know the classic dim sum items that you should try when you're in Hong Kong.

Char siu bao: A firm favourite, the soft fluffy steamed bun has a filling of rich, savoury Cantonese barbecue pork. Some experts believe a perfect char siu bao must split open or 'smile'.

Char siu sou: Brushed with egg and sprinkled with sesame seeds, this baked morsel of flaky pastry made with lard is filled with tender char siu. Triangular-shaped, it's as much a sight to behold as a joy to eat. A superior *char siu sou* is rich and must be served warm.

Cheong fun: Made with rice flour, this steamed snowy-white roll made with various fillings is universally loved. Typical fillings include char siu, minced beef and prawns, and, in a vegetarian version called *zaa leong*, fried cruller, or dough. These rolls are served with sweetened soy sauce and a drizzle of oil.

Dan tat: If you love a custard tart, this sublime Cantonese version is a must. Said to have originated from the English or Portuguese tart, this treat with sweet silky-smooth custard with just that bit of wobble encased in puff or short pastry often marks the end of a meal (see page 222).

Fung zao: Known as 'phoenix talons' in Cantonese, these chicken feet dim sum hit the scene internationally in the 1960s. Maybe an acquired taste, the feet are fried, then simmered with fermented black beans and chilli until meltingly gelatinous and juicy.

Ham sui gok: A football-shaped deep-fried beauty made of sticky-rice flour and wheat starch with hints of sugar, and filled with savoury pork, this crisp, chewy dumpling is admired for its pastry. Properly executed, it's irresistible, with none of the lingering oily taste of inferior versions.

Har gao: The work of a master dim sum chef, this is a dumpling of prawns and bamboo shoot wrapped with a skin made of wheat starch and tapioca flour. It must have at least nine pleats to prove the chef's prowess.

Lai wong bao: This popular steamed sweet bun, always eaten warm, has a soft, buttery custard in the centre. This classic has a relatively recent rival called lava bao or *lau sa bao*, meaning 'flowing-sand bun'. This creation yields a rich sweet-salty molten filling of butter and salted egg yolks. Delicious.

Lo bak gou: Also known as 'radish cake', this favourite is made with grated daikon radish, rice-flour batter, shiitake mushrooms, lap cheong sausage, dried shrimp and fried shallots. It's steamed in a mould, cooled and then sliced before being pan-fried to yield a crisp crust and creamy interior.

Loh mai gai: Wrapped in lotus leaf for its unique fragrance, this dim sum of steamed glutinous rice, chicken, shiitake, lap cheong, dried shrimp and sometimes roast duck is heavenly.

Si jup jing pai gwat: This Cantonese classic of steamed pork spare ribs with chillies and fermented black beans is a perfect foil to the dumplings and buns. These should be tender and succulent.

Siu long bao: Better known as *xiao long bao*, this steamed dumpling from the ancient town of Nanxiang on the outskirts of Shanghai has a history of more than 100 years and is renowned for its thin skin encasing juicy pork and umami-packed broth. Made properly, it is a revelation.

Siu mai: This classic open-faced steamed dumpling contains chopped pork and prawns wrapped in wonton pastry. Richer fillings include shiitake mushrooms and abalone. Some older establishments serve *siu mai* topped with liver, called *ju yuen siu mai*.

So pei char siu bao: Made famous by Tim Ho Wan's dim sum master Mak Kwai Pui, these soft barbecue pork buns have a crackly sugar topping. You will savour the memory long after you've tried one of these creations.

Wo tip: The Cantonese equivalent of the Shanghainese *guotie* and Japanese *gyoza*, this pan-fried pork dumpling with its more resilient pastry is known in the West as a pot-sticker. Often eaten with red rice vinegar, the perfect *wo tip* must have a crisp base to contrast its succulent filling.

Wu gok: Another work of art, these gossamer-like deep-fried taro dumplings shaped like an egg are filled with minced pork, prawns and dried shrimps, and accented with Chinese five-spice. Look out for just-cooked taro dumplings, which are initially brittle, then soft before yielding to a meaty juicy filling.

Steamed pork and prawn dumplings

Makes 25-30

These open-faced steamed dumplings are traditionally made with minced pork and wrapped with wonton pastry. Known as *siu mai*, meaning 'cook and sell dumplings', they're said to be from Inner Mongolia originally, but the Cantonese have made them remarkably delicious.

Siu mai are easy to make, but you need to create their characteristic 'bounce'. To achieve this, run-of-the-mill yum cha places tend to use lots of pork fat, which, to me, is unhealthy and unpleasant. I like to use a ratio of 80 per cent lean meat to 20 per cent fat so that the dumplings don't taste dry. Good yum cha restaurants use a combination of pork and prawns in the filling to create the bounce effect, as I have done here. Uncooked *siu mai* dumplings can be frozen for up to 2 weeks.

25–30 square wonton wrappers
2 tablespoons finely chopped carrot

FILLING
2 dried shiitake mushrooms, soaked in hot water
    until softened
300 g (10½ oz) pork belly, coarsely chopped
180 g (6½ oz) peeled uncooked prawns,
    coarsely chopped
80 g (2¾ oz) water chestnuts, chopped
2 tablespoons light soy sauce
1½ tablespoons Shaoxing rice wine
2 teaspoons sesame oil
2 tablespoons finely chopped ginger
1 spring onion (scallion), thinly sliced
1 egg white
2 tablespoons potato flour

To make the filling, squeeze the excess water from the mushrooms, discard the stems and finely chop the caps. Combine the mushrooms in a large bowl with the remaining ingredients, season with salt and pepper and mix well. (Dim sum chefs tend to stir the mixture in one direction 20 times.) Cover the bowl with plastic wrap and set aside for 20 minutes to marinate.

Place a teaspoonful of filling in the centre of each wrapper. Bring up the sides and gently squeeze to hold in the filling. Smooth the top of the filling with a knife and gently tap the bottoms of the dumplings on the bench so they stand upright. Top each dumpling with a pinch of carrot.

Line a bamboo steamer with baking paper and make a few tiny slits to allow the steam to rise through. Or lightly brush the steamer with oil. Steam the dumplings in batches for 8–10 minutes or until cooked through. Serve at once.

Note
Dim sum chefs tend to cut off the square edges of the wrappers for aesthetics but this is not necessary.

Steamed glutinous rice parcels in lotus leaves

A yum cha favourite called *loh mai gai*, these classic Cantonese parcels of glutinous rice, diced chicken, lap cheong sausage and shiitake mushrooms wrapped in lotus leaf are also great for snacks and light lunches. The method looks long, but this recipe is easy to make.

250 g (9 oz) skinless chicken, diced
5 lotus leaves (see Note)
600 g (1 lb 5 oz) glutinous rice,
    soaked overnight in cold water
    and drained
4 tablespoons vegetable oil
4 dried shiitake mushrooms, soaked
    in hot water and drained
1 tablespoon dried shrimp, soaked in
    4 tablespoons hot water
100 g (3½ oz) barbecue pork
    (char siu), diced
2 lap cheong sausages, thinly sliced

185 ml (6 fl oz/¾ cup) chicken stock
1 tablespoon cornflour (cornstarch)

MARINADE
1 tablespoon oyster sauce
2 teaspoons Shaoxing rice wine
1 teaspoon dark soy sauce
1 tablespoon light soy sauce
2 teaspoons ginger juice
    (see Note)
1 teaspoon sesame oil
1 teaspoon sugar
½ teaspoon pepper

Mix the marinade ingredients in a bowl, add the chicken, mix to coat well and refrigerate for 30 minutes. Meanwhile, soak the lotus leaves in boiling water for 30 minutes or until pliable. Drain the leaves and pat dry with paper towel. Cut into quarters, trim and set aside.

Line a large bamboo steamer with a sheet of baking paper. Spread the rice over the paper, cover and steam for 30–40 minutes over a saucepan of simmering water until tender. Transfer the rice to a bowl, add 2 tablespoons of the oil, mix well and cover with a tea towel.

Squeeze the excess water from the mushrooms, discard the stems and dice the caps. Drain the shrimp, reserving the liquid. Heat the remaining oil in a wok, add the mushrooms, shrimp, pork and lap cheong and stir-fry for 1 minute. Add the chicken and fry for a further 2–3 minutes. Stir in the chicken stock and bring to the boil. Mix the cornflour with the reserved shrimp liquid, add to the chicken mixture and stir until thickened. Season to taste with salt and white pepper and leave to cool completely.

With lightly oiled hands, divide the rice into 20–24 balls. Place a rice ball in the centre of a lotus leaf and flatten. Top with 2 tablespoons of filling, then another portion of rice and flatten. Fold the bottom third of the leaf over the rice, then fold in the sides and roll up to form a parcel. Repeat with remaining rice, filling and lotus leaves. Arrange the parcels in a steamer and cook over high heat for 20–30 minutes. Serve hot.

Note

Dried lotus leaves are available from Asian grocers. To make ginger juice, pound or grate a 5 cm (2 inch) piece of ginger, place in muslin and squeeze juice into a bowl.

Scallop and chive dumplings

These delectable dumplings come from Li Shu Tim, the dim sum chef at One Harbour Road. The filling includes doubanjiang, the spicy chilli sauce from Sichuan province, but only a touch – Cantonese diners don't like their food too hot. The pastry is fascinating. Made with wheat starch and tapioca flour, it's a bit involved, but once you've made it the first time it becomes much easier. Part of the dough mixture is made with boiling water, which in some ways is similar to the hot-water pastry used for British meat pies. This recipe makes more pastry than you need, but it will keep in the fridge, wrapped in plastic. If you don't feel like making the pastry, just buy *gow gee* dumpling skins from your Asian grocer.

FILLING
120 g (4¼ oz) garlic chives
1 teaspoon tapioca flour
70 g (2½ oz) uncooked prawn meat
220 g (7¾ oz) scallops without roe, diced
1 teaspoon vegetable oil
2 teaspoons caster (superfine) sugar
2 teaspoons doubanjiang

PASTRY A
210 g (7½ oz) tapioca flour
70 g (2½ oz) wheat starch

PASTRY B
210 g (7½ oz) wheat starch
70 g (2½ oz) tapioca flour

To make the filling, put 500 ml (17 fl oz/2 cups) water in a small saucepan and bring to the boil. Add the chives for 20 seconds, then drain and refresh in iced water. Pat dry and chop into 1 cm (½ inch) lengths. Add ½ teaspoon tapioca flour and a pinch of salt and to the prawn meat and stir in one direction for 2 minutes. Refrigerate for 10–15 minutes (this is a Chinese technique to make the prawns crunchy). Rinse the prawns under cold water to remove the starch. Pat dry with paper towel and chop into a small dice similar in size to the scallops.

Put the prawns, scallops, vegetable oil, sugar, doubanjiang, chives and remaining tapioca flour in a bowl. Season with 1 teaspoon salt and white pepper and mix well. Refrigerate until needed.

For the pastry, mix the tapioca flour and wheat starch from pastry A in an electric mixer, add 500 ml (17 fl oz/2 cups) boiling water and mix quickly. Once formed into a dough, mix in the wheat starch and tapioca flour from pastry B, turn out onto a clean work surface and knead for 3–5 minutes until combined.

Form the dough into a long roll and cut into equal portions of around 20 g (¾ oz). Roll each out to a disc of 8–10 cm (3½–4 inches) diameter. Place a teaspoonful of filling in the centre of each, then fold and pinch the edges together to form a dumpling. Steam the dumplings for 6 minutes and serve with your choice of dipping sauce.

Steamed beef balls

Makes 20

One of my earliest experiences of a traditional Hong Kong teahouse was visiting the legendary Lin Heung. You come to this rough-and-tumble institution, packed to the rafters since it opened in 1926, to soak up the atmosphere of old Hong Kong. The dim sum make no concessions to modernity – servings are hefty though authentic. On offer might be these popular steamed beef balls, perfumed with dried tangerine peel and much appreciated for their soft mousse-like texture and bouncy mouthfeel. It's a simple recipe, particularly if you have a food processor. To keep faith with authenticity, I've included pork fat and bicarbonate of soda, but leave these out if you prefer. Should you decide to leave out pork fat, increase the weight of beef. The dish is typically served with Worcestershire sauce – an unusual but delicious contribution from British cookery.

1 piece dried tangerine peel
400 g (14 oz) minced (ground) beef
60 g (2¼ oz) pork fat, cooked and minced
2 teaspoons ginger juice, squeezed from
    grated fresh ginger
1 tablespoon light soy sauce
½ teaspoon sugar
½ teaspoon bicarbonate of soda (baking soda)
1 small egg white, lightly beaten
1 tablespoon cornflour (cornstarch) mixed with 125 ml
    (4 fl oz/½ cup) water
1 spring onion (scallion), finely chopped

Soak the tangerine peel in warm water for 15 minutes, then drain and finely chop. It should yield 1 tablespoonful. Combine the chopped peel with the beef and pork fat in a food processor and process to a paste. If you prefer a coarser texture, use the pulse action (see Note). Transfer to a large bowl, add the remaining ingredients and season with salt and white pepper. Mix well, cover with plastic wrap and refrigerate for 1 hour.

When ready to serve, dampen your hands with a little vegetable oil. Form the beef mixture into walnut-sized balls and place in a heatproof dish. Put the dish in a bamboo basket and steam over rapidly boiling water for 8–12 minutes or until cooked. Serve with Worcestershire sauce or your favourite dipping sauce.

Note *Traditionally, the beef mixture is worked very intensely by slapping it against the side of a bowl to develop the bouncy texture. Sometimes these beef balls are steamed over cabbage leaves or bean curd sheets.*

Radish cake

Serves 6-10

This popular dim sum, called *lo bak gou*, is served during Chinese New Year as a symbol of rising fortunes, but it's also found at yum cha houses throughout the year. I don't know why this savoury cake or pudding is called turnip cake when it is, in fact, made with Chinese radish or daikon. Chinese conundrum! It's easy to make and often served fried. Although radish cake can be served hot, it's often cooled and refrigerated until it's firm. It's then sliced into portions and fried until it's slightly crisp. Many dim sum chefs blanch the radish before making the cake to remove the slightly bitter taste, but I find the flavour is lost in the process.

600 g (1 lb 5 oz) peeled daikon
1 tablespoon Shaoxing rice wine
6–8 dried shiitake mushrooms, soaked in 250 ml
    (9 fl oz/1 cup) hot water until softened
30 g (1 oz) dried shrimp, soaked in 3 tablespoons
    hot water for 20 minutes
2 tablespoons vegetable oil
2 lap cheong sausages (see Note), finely diced
2 spring onions (scallions), thinly sliced
1 teaspoon caster (superfine) sugar
250 g (9 oz) rice flour
30 g (1 oz) potato or cornflour (cornstarch)
375 ml (13 fl oz/1½ cups) chicken stock
Thinly sliced spring onions (scallion) and your choice
    of dipping sauce, to serve

Grate the daikon into a bowl and add the rice wine. Set aside. Drain the mushrooms, reserving the soaking liquid, squeeze the excess moisture from the mushrooms, discard the stems and thinly slice the caps. Drain the dried shrimp, reserving the soaking liquid.

Heat the oil in a wok and fry the diced sausages until fragrant. Add the mushrooms, dried shrimp and spring onions, and fry for another 1–2 minutes. Set aside.

Combine the daikon, sugar, 1 teaspoon each salt and white pepper and 125 ml (4 fl oz/½ cup) water in a saucepan and cook over medium–low heat for 10–15 minutes until daikon is soft and the water is almost evaporated.

Meanwhile, mix the rice flour and potato flour or cornflour together in a bowl. Add the stock and the reserved liquid from the mushrooms and shrimp. Mix to a smooth batter, then stir in the hot radish and sausage mixtures. The radish needs to be hot to partially cook the flours and form a sticky mess.

Pour the mixture into an oiled 28 cm (11¼ inch) round cake tin and steam over a saucepan of rapidly boiling for 30–40 minutes until an inserted skewer comes out clean (Chinese cooks place a tea towel over the cake to absorb the condensation while it's cooking). Rest for 5 minutes, cut into squares, garnish with spring onions and serve with dipping sauce.

Note *Chinese bacon can be used in place of the lap cheong.*

Char siu bao (barbecue pork buns)

Makes 22

One of the most famed items at any Chinese dim sum establishment, *char siu bao*, especially the steamed variety, is a long-time favourite. These soft, fluffy steamed buns with their characteristic three-pointed split on top are filled with salty-sweet barbecued pork. They are easy enough to make, although the dough can be tricky; traditionally it's made with a kind of Chinese sourdough starter called *lao mian* that contains a dash of food-grade lye water (potassium carbonate) and ammonia carbonate, a leavening agent also used in traditional recipes from northern Europe and Italy. Dim sum chefs use Hong Kong flour for this dough, a finely milled soft wheat flour with a low gluten content. It's sold in some Chinese grocers, but any cake flour will work well. This recipe doesn't use lye water or ammonia carbonate and consequently the buns don't split like the *char siu bao* you see at dim sum eateries, but it works a treat and is easy to make, especially with a bread-making machine. You can cheat by using the ready-made bao flour sold at Chinese supermarkets. Once you've grasped the technique, you'll make these signature Cantonese steamed buns again and again.

BARBECUE PORK FILLING
200 ml (7 fl oz) chicken stock
30 g (1 oz) caster (superfine) sugar
2 tablespoons oyster sauce
1 tablespoon light soy sauce
1 teaspoon dark soy sauce
2 tablespoons vegetable oil
2 garlic cloves, finely chopped
2 small red Asian shallots, finely chopped
1 tablespoon finely chopped ginger
1 tablespoon finely chopped spring onions (scallions),
    white part only
3 tablespoons cornflour (cornstarch) mixed with
    100 ml (3½ fl oz) water
300 g (10½ oz) barbecue pork (see page 62),
    finely diced

BAO DOUGH
60 g (2¼ oz) caster (superfine) sugar
250 ml (9 fl oz/1 cup) lukewarm water
1½ teaspoons dried yeast
430 g (15¼ oz) cake flour
3 teaspoons baking powder
2 tablespoons vegetable oil
½ teaspoon rice vinegar

To make the filling, combine the chicken stock, sugar, oyster sauce and soy sauces in a jug. Mix well and set aside. Heat the oil in a wok over high heat, add the garlic, shallots, ginger, spring onions and fry until just golden. Add the stock mixture, bring to the boil, then reduce heat and simmer for about 5 minutes.

Stir in the cornflour mixture and stir continuously until thickened. Add the pork, stir to combine, then transfer to a bowl and leave to cool completely.

To make the dough, dissolve the sugar in the lukewarm water, stir in the yeast and set aside in a draught-free place for 10 minutes until it turns foamy.

Sift the flour and baking powder into a bowl. Make a well in the centre, add the yeast mixture, oil, vinegar and a pinch of salt, then, using a wooden spoon, stir until well combined. Turn out onto a lightly floured bench and knead for 8–10 minutes until the dough is soft and pliable (this can also be done in an electric mixer with a dough hook attachment).

Place the dough in a lightly oiled bowl, turn to coat evenly, cover with plastic wrap or a tea towel, and set aside in a draught-free place until doubled in size (1–2 hours or up to 3–4 hours on a cold day).

Punch down the dough and turn out onto a lightly floured surface. Cut the dough in half. Cover one piece with a tea towel, roll the other into a cylinder and cut into 11 equal pieces. Roll each piece into a ball, then into a 15 cm (6 inch) diameter round. Repeat with remaining dough.

Cut out twenty-two 20 cm-square pieces of baking paper. Hold a round of dough in your cupped hand and spoon a tablespoonful of filling into the centre. Gather the dough around the filling, pinch the edges together to form a bun and twist gently to seal. Place on a square of baking paper and repeat with remaining dough and filling.

Cover the buns with a tea towel and set aside until risen slightly (30 minutes to 1 hour). Steam the buns in batches, covered, in a steamer over a saucepan of boiling water until puffed and cooked through (12–15 minutes). Serve hot.

Note *Steamed buns can be frozen for 2 weeks.*

Baked barbecue pork buns

Walking into a Chinese bakery can be overwhelming. Faced with stacks of steamed and baked buns in all shapes and sizes, not to mention their myriad fillings, it makes for difficult choices. But the great thing is that most of the pastries are made from the same basic dough. These barbecue pork buns, for instance, use the same pastry as the pineapple buns on page 220, but here the barbecue pork (char siu) combines with the sweetish pastry to create savoury buns. Some Chinese bakeries leave out the crunchy topping I've used here, while others add chopped onions to the filling. Baked barbecue pork buns, called *char siu sou*, are pretty common in Cantonese bakeries.

BARBECUE PORK FILLING
200 ml (7 fl oz) chicken stock
30 g (1 oz) sugar
1 tablespoon light soy sauce
1 teaspoon dark soy sauce
2 tablespoons oyster sauce
2 tablespoons vegetable oil
1 tablespoon finely chopped ginger
1 tablespoon finely chopped spring onion (scallion), white part only
2 small red Asian shallots, finely chopped
2 garlic cloves, finely chopped
3 tablespoons cornflour (cornstarch), mixed with 100 ml (3½ fl oz) water
300 g (10½ oz) barbecue pork (char siu), finely diced

WATER ROUX
50 g (1¾ oz) plain (all-purpose) flour

BUN DOUGH
2 teaspoons dried yeast
50 g (1¾ oz) caster (superfine) sugar
½ quantity water roux
3½ tablespoons milk
300 g (10½ oz) plain (all-purpose) flour
1 egg, beaten
30 g (1 oz) butter, softened

TOPPING
110 g (3¾ oz) butter
100 g (3½ oz) caster (superfine) sugar
2 egg yolks
190 g (6¾ oz) plain (all-purpose) flour
½ teaspoon baking powder
½ teaspoon bicarbonate of soda (baking soda)
1 egg, beaten with 2 tablespoons water, for eggwash

Continued overleaf

To make the barbecue pork filling, put the chicken stock, sugar, soy sauces and oyster sauce in a small bowl and mix well. Heat a wok over medium–high heat and add the oil. Add the ginger, spring onions, shallots and garlic and fry until just golden, then add the stock mixture and bring to the boil. Reduce the heat to a simmer and cook for about 5 minutes.

Add the cornflour mixture and stir until thickened, then add the pork. Season with a pinch of salt. Remove from the wok and leave to cool completely.

To make the water roux, put the flour in a saucepan with 250 ml (9 fl oz/1 cup) water and whisk to combine, ensuring there are no lumps. Stir over medium–low heat for 2–3 minutes until the mixture thickens to the consistency of a béchamel sauce or reaches 65°C (150°F). Remove from the heat, cover the surface with plastic wrap to prevent it drying out and refrigerate. Bring to room temperature before using. The roux should be used within 3 days.

To make the bun dough, combine the yeast, 1½ tablespoons water and 1 teaspoon of the sugar in a cup and leave until foamy. Place in an electric mixer fitted with a dough hook with a half-quantity of the water roux, the remaining dough ingredients and ½ teaspoon salt. Knead on the lowest speed for about 10–15 minutes until smooth. Put the dough in a lightly oiled bowl, cover with a tea towel and leave in a draught-free place for 1–2 hours until doubled in size.

Meanwhile, to make the topping, beat the butter and sugar until pale and creamy. Beat in the egg yolks, then beat in the remaining ingredients and a pinch of salt. Form the mixture into a roll on a sheet of baking paper, roll up and refrigerate until firm. Cut into 16 portions.

Knock back the dough and divide into 16 portions. Roll each piece into a ball, then into a 15 cm (6 inch) diameter round.

Cut out sixteen 20 cm (8 inch) squares of baking paper. Hold a round of dough in your cupped hand and spoon a tablespoonful of filling into the centre. Gather the dough around the filling, pinch the edges together to form a bun and twist gently to seal. Place on a square of baking paper. Once all the buns are filled, cover with a tea towel and leave to rise for 30 minutes.

Preheat the oven to 190°C (375°F). Flatten the topping portions into thin discs and place each on a bun to just cover. Brush with eggwash and bake for 5 minutes, then reduce the oven to 180°C (350°F) and bake for another 10 minutes or until the buns are well risen and golden. Serve warm.

Lava bao

This recent addition to the yum cha repertoire is one of the most exciting creations. Called *lau sa bao* in Cantonese, meaning 'flowing sand', this steamed bao is filled with a savoury-sweet custard made with salted duck yolks, butter and milk. On paper, this might sound odd, but after you've tried the delicious runny custard you'll be an addict. Split the preparation over 2 days and you'll be surprised how easy it is to make it. If you love molten chocolate cake, I think you'll like this bao, too. Salted duck egg yolks are found in the freezer section of Asian grocers, or make your own (see page 247).

CUSTARD
150 g (5½ oz) salted duck egg yolks
125 g (4½ oz) salted butter, softened
2 tablespoons custard powder
3 tablespoons milk powder
100 ml (3½ fl oz) evaporated milk
250 g (9 oz) icing sugar

BAO DOUGH
5 g (⅛ oz) active dry yeast
300 g (10½ oz) plain (all-purpose) flour
50 g (1¾ oz) caster (superfine) sugar
1 teaspoon baking powder
2 tablespoons vegetable oil

To make the custard, steam the yolks in a steamer over a saucepan of simmering water for 5 minutes or until cooked. Leave to cool, then process in a food processor to a crumbly powder. Transfer to a bowl and add the butter, custard powder and milk powder. Mix well, then add the evaporated milk and icing sugar. Mix until combined, then cover and freeze until solid.

Working quickly, using an ice-cream scoop or a tablespoon, form the frozen custard mixture into 20 g (¾ oz) balls. Place them on a tray lined with baking paper and freeze again until solid.

To make the bao dough, sprinkle the yeast onto 125 ml (4 fl oz/½ cup) warm water, between 32°C and 35°C (90°F and 95°F) and leave until foamy. Combine the flour, sugar and baking powder in a bowl. Add the yeast and oil and knead until smooth (15–20 minutes, or 10 minutes in an electric mixer fitted with a dough hook). Divide the dough into 30 portions. Roll each into a ball and flatten to form a round about 1 cm (½ inch) thick.

Place a custard portion in the centre of each round of dough and gather up the sides to form a ball. Pinch to close and transfer seam-side down to paper cupcake liners sprayed with non-stick spray.

Leave to rise for 40 minutes until doubled in size. Steam in batches in a bamboo steamer over a saucepan of simmering water for 6–8 minutes until cooked through. Cool for 5 minutes before serving (or the filling will be explosively hot).

desserts and pastries

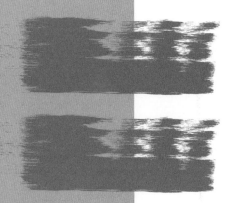

WHEN CHRIS PATTEN, HONG KONG'S LAST BRITISH GOVERNOR, DECLARED A LIKING FOR DAN TAT (EGG TARTS), HE GENERATED A CULINARY TSUNAMI IN THE WESTERN WORLD.

Why? Because most people in the West didn't associate Chinese food with cakes and pastries. Patten initiated an international pastry pilgrimage to his favourite baker, the Tai Cheong Bakery in Central, and forever changed the perception of Chinese sweets.

What are Chinese sweets? Not much has been written in English about their provenance. Some Chinese cookbooks trace their origins to China's Three Kingdoms period (AD 220–280). Others suggest they came into vogue when teahouses were established during the Tang dynasty (AD 618–907). And social historians claim that Chinese sweet pastries have always been around because they're served at birthdays, weddings and other celebrations.

In Hong Kong there are Chinese pastry shops everywhere. The old-school neighbourhood bakery occupies a special place in the hearts of locals – it's where they go for daily pastries and celebration cakes alike. Some, such as Hang Heung and Kee Wah bakeries, are more traditional and offer delicacies such as wife's cakes and moon cakes filled with fudge-like lotus seeds and red beans. Others, like Tai Cheong and Hoover Cake Shop, are more innovative and offer Western-style treats such as Swiss rolls and tarts along with time-honoured nutty moon cakes, peanut mochi, dragon's beard candy and savoury chicken biscuits (*gai zai peang*).

While no one knows exactly when a new breed of Hong Kong bakery starting offering Western-style baked treats, one thing is certain: Chinese pastries run the full gamut of cooking techniques and can include surprising

ingredients. Who would think of wedging a slice of pungent century egg into a sweet pastry (*pei daan so*), or turning savoury fermented bean curd into a chewy treat and calling it chicken biscuit? Or that lard would make the best-tasting pastry for sweet Chinese-style egg tarts?

I believe Hong Kong's pastry cooks are in a unique position. Combining their knowledge of Chinese pastry culture with influences from the British and the Portuguese, they've created pastries that are uniquely theirs: the ubiquitous egg tart, the cocktail bun or *gai mei bao*, a soft bread bun filled with coconut, and the pineapple bun or *bo lo bao*, a treat with a sugary crust but no pineapple, among others.

Hong Kong now has posh bakeries that wouldn't look out of place in Paris or New York, but for an affordable and nostalgic teatime snack, nothing beats the old-time modest bakeries that are part and parcel of the city's culture.

Sweets aren't necessarily served at the close of a meal – they're enjoyed between meals or even in the middle of one. I'm still stunned by a Chiu Chow dish of fried crisp noodles sprinkled with vinegar and eaten between courses with masses of sugar.

Desserts are often simple because we don't like rich foods at the end of a meal. Traditional desserts may be nothing more than lotus seeds, birds' nests or gingko nuts cooked in sugar syrup because they're thought to balance the yin and yang of our bodies. For instance, the Chinese believe black sesame with gingko reduces hair loss and promotes longevity.

Mention dessert at the end of a meal and most Chinese people will think of either fresh fruit or a bowl of sweetened almond soup, but in Hong Kong there's a distinct dessert culture. Locals love their sweets and dessert restaurants stretch from Chai Wan in the east to Yuen Long in the north-west. Known as *tong shui* (meaning sugar water) or *tim bun* (dessert) shops, they're the destinations for a sugar hit.

Yee Shun Milk Company is one out of the bag. An old-school *cha chaan teng* ('tea restaurant'), it features puddings made with milk. Considering fresh cow's milk is not typically part of the Chinese diet, these are a wonder to savour, and a lovely surprise even for a regular visitor to Hong Kong like me. Condensed and evaporated milks feature extensively in traditional Cantonese desserts, but fresh milk is rare.

Most of the traditional shops are buzzy and family-friendly, with little attention given to décor, and the sweet treats are typically Cantonese. They're well priced and the dishes are presented simply. Now a new generation of chefs has given local sweets a makeover. Combining nuts, seeds and seasonal fruits such as mangoes, durian and lychees with Western techniques, their sweets tend to be refreshing and light.

Dessert houses such as Honeymoon Dessert, Auntie Sweet and Lucky Dessert are popular with both locals and visitors. Snow ice, for instance, made with fruit syrup and milk, is the hot-ticket item at these places and a must-try. Ice creams made with green tea, red bean and taro are regular items and are often combined with soft tofu and syrup.

Expect also to find grass jelly, made with a member of the mint family, served with chewy tapioca balls in the menu selection. Servings tend to be extremely generous – Kei Kee Dessert's famed B Boy grass jelly is a classic example.

Brian Lam and Dominic Li's Dessert Kitchen with its utterly delicious creations has seen queues ever since it opened in 2006 (it now has around 30 outposts extending as far as Australia). And Lab Made Ice Cream, although not a dessert joint, offers some of the most intriguing ingredients in its liquid-nitrogen ice cream such as purple rice and salted duck yolk custard.

Hong Kong desserts have come a long way from the days of simple flavours and ingredients. There's still a tendency to have food based on heating and cooling (yin–yang) principles, but the locals have adapted with the times. Traditional ingredients are presented with panache and ice creams with local flavourings are regular features. Once you get the hang of these desserts, the glory of Hong Kong sweets will certainly be part of your kitchen repertoire.

Chilled mango, sago, pomelo and coconut soup

This is one of the most refreshing desserts for summer. Apparently it was invented by a chef from the Lei Garden restaurant group in the mid-1980s. In Chinese it's called 'dropping manna from a willow branch' – a reference to the vase with a willow branch held by the Goddess of Mercy. Over the years, it has evolved and some dessert-only shops such as Lucky Dessert serve it with ice cream. Pomelo is a giant, soccer-balled-sized fruit, rather like an orange but twenty sizes large. Cut around the rind and then rip the flesh apart into individual juice sacs. If you love chilled fruit soups, this is a must. Serve it in a dessert glass and wait for the compliments from your guests.

110 g (3¾ oz/½ cup) caster (superfine) sugar
90 g (3¼ oz/½ cup) sago
3 ripe mangoes, peeled, seeded and diced
1 litre (35 fl oz/4 cups) coconut milk
1 cupful pomelo sacs, plus extra to serve

Put the sugar and 125 ml (4 fl oz/½ cup) water into a small saucepan, bring to a simmer and stir until the sugar has completely dissolved. Cool, then chill until required.

Bring 1 litre (35 fl oz/4 cups) water to the boil in a saucepan. Slowly trickle in the sago, ensuring the water remains on the boil. Boil, stirring occasionally, for 7 minutes. Remove from the heat, cover with a lid and set aside for 20 minutes to finish cooking – the sago will become translucent. Pour it into a fine sieve and rinse off the excess starch under cold running water. Refrigerate until required.

Combine 2 of the mangoes in a blender with the chilled sugar syrup and coconut milk and process until smooth. Transfer to a bowl and stir in the sago and pomelo sacs. Chill until required.

Spoon into serving glasses and top with diced mango and extra pomelo.

Mango puddings

This delicious pudding, which I suspect is adapted from an English recipe,
is a staple at dim sum restaurants. Delicate and light, it's best made with fresh
mangoes but, at a pinch, tinned mango purée can be used. It's effortless to make
and perfect for a Sunday brunch or Chinese feast.

200 g (7 oz) caster (superfine) sugar
30 g (1 oz) powdered gelatine, sprinkled over
   3 tablespoons water
500 g (1 lb 2 oz) mango flesh, puréed
250 ml (9 fl oz/1 cup) evaporated milk
125 ml (4 fl oz/½ cup) coconut milk
Sliced strawberries, to serve

Put 1 litre (35 fl oz/4 cups) water and the sugar in a saucepan, bring to the boil
and simmer gently, stirring until the sugar has dissolved. Add the gelatine and
continue simmering, stirring, until completely dissolved. Cool for 5 minutes.

   Combine the mango purée, evaporated milk and coconut milk in a bowl,
then stir in the gelatine mixture. Pour into 125 ml (4 fl oz/½ cup) moulds and
refrigerate for 5 hours until set. Unmould the puddings onto plates and
serve with strawberries.

Bo lo bao (pineapple buns)

Hong Kong originals, these buns are such an intrinsic part of the city's life that the government has given them cultural-heritage status. Made with a soft, sweet dough and crowned with a sugary crust, they contain no pineapple – the name refers to the cracked surface that resembles the 'eyes' of a pineapple. They're often enjoyed as a snack with a cup of tea, sometimes with a pat of butter slipped inside. I often wondered how Asian breads were so soft and pillowy, until I found a recipe by Hong Kong chef May Chow that explained *tong zhong*, as it's called in Cantonese. The mystery was solved; in this Asian technique, flour and water are cooked to 65°C (150°F) to make a water 'roux', which locks moisture into the dough and renders it super-soft.

50 g (1¾ oz) plain (all-purpose) flour
2 teaspoons (7 g) dried yeast
50 g (1¾ oz) caster (superfine) sugar
70 ml (2¼ fl oz) milk
300 g (10½ oz/2 cups) plain
   (all-purpose) flour
1 egg, beaten
30 g (1 oz) butter, softened

TOPPING
110 g (3¾ oz) butter
100 g (3¾ oz) caster (superfine)
   sugar
2 egg yolks
190 g (6¾ oz) plain (all-purpose)
   flour
½ teaspoon baking powder
½ teaspoon baking soda
1 teaspoon vanilla essence
1 egg, beaten with 2 tablespoons
   water, for eggwash

To make the water roux, put the flour in a saucepan with 250 ml (9 fl oz/1 cup) water and whisk until smooth. Stir over medium–low heat for 2–3 minutes until the mixture thickens to the consistency of a béchamel or reaches 65°C (150°F). Remove from the heat, cover the surface with plastic wrap to prevent it drying out and refrigerate. Bring to room temperature before using. The roux should be used within 3 days.

Mix the yeast, 1 teaspoon of the sugar and 1½ tablespoons water in a cup and leave until frothy. Combine the yeast mixture in an electric mixer fitted with a dough hook with a half-quantity of the water roux, the remaining ingredients and ½ teaspoon salt. Knead on the lowest speed for 10–15 minutes until smooth. Transfer the dough to a lightly oiled bowl, cover with a tea towel and set aside in a draught-free place for 1–2 hours until doubled in size.

Meanwhile, to make the topping, beat the butter and sugar until pale and creamy. Beat in the egg yolks, then beat in the remaining ingredients and a pinch of salt. Form the mixture into a roll on a sheet of baking paper, roll up and refrigerate until firm. Cut into 16 portions.

Knock back the dough, divide into 16 portions and roll each into a ball. Place on a baking tray lined with baking paper. Cover and leave to rise for 30 minutes.

Preheat the oven to 190°C (375°F). Flatten the topping portions into thin discs and place each on a bun to just cover. Brush with eggwash and bake for 5 minutes, then reduce the oven to 180°C (350°F) and bake for a further 10 minutes or until well risen and golden. Cool before eating.

Dan tat (egg tarts)

Considered to be a legacy of the Portuguese and British, these ubiquitous Cantonese custard tarts have been around since the 1940s. They were made famous by the last British governor, Chris Patten, who declared Tai Cheong Bakery's tarts the best in the world. They're usually made with short pastry, although some bakeries, such as the Honolulu Coffee Shop in Wan Chai, make them with puff pastry.

SHORT PASTRY
225 g (8 oz) plain (all-purpose) flour, plus extra
   for dusting
50 g (1¾ oz) caster (superfine) sugar
110 g (3¾ oz) cold butter, cut into small cubes

CUSTARD FILLING
120 g (4¼ oz) caster (superfine) sugar
2 eggs, lightly beaten
100 ml (3½ fl oz) evaporated milk
½ teaspoon vanilla essence

To make the pastry, combine the flour, sugar and butter on a work surface and lightly rub with your fingers to partly combine. Make a well in the centre and add 2 tablespoons cold water. Using a pastry scraper, work the mixture into a buttery dough. Smear the dough away from you with the heel of your hand, then gather together and form it into a flat disc. Dust lightly with flour, wrap in plastic wrap and refrigerate for 20–30 minutes to rest.

To make the custard, put the sugar and 225 ml (7¾ fl oz) water in a small saucepan. Bring to the boil, stirring until the sugar has dissolved, then set aside to cool. Combine the eggs, evaporated milk and vanilla essence in a bowl, stir in the cooled sugar syrup and mix well without creating bubbles. Strain the mixture through a fine sieve into a jug.

Preheat the oven to 200°C (400°F). Roll out the pastry on a lightly floured bench to a thickness of 5 mm (¼ inch). Using a fluted cookie cutter a little larger than your tart cases (see Note), cut the dough into rounds. Ease the pastry rounds into the buttered cases, transfer to the oven rack and pour the custard into the pastry cases.

Bake for 12–15 minutes or until the edges are lightly browned, then reduce the heat to 180°C (350°F) and carefully rotate the tray. Continue to bake for 10 minutes or until the custard is slightly puffed. Cool for 10 minutes before removing the tarts from their cases.

Note *I used 6 cm (2½ inch) pastry cases. Any leftover pastry can be frozen for up to a month.*

Green-tea ice cream

Hong Kong is obsessed with green-tea or matcha ice cream. On a hot summer's day, you'll find matcha lovers tucking into this ice cream with the likes of sponge cakes, chocolate sauce, chestnut cream – the list goes on. One of the best versions is found at Via Tokyo in Causeway Bay. Just be prepared to queue. I like to serve this with diced mango or lychee.

450 ml (16 fl oz) milk
250 ml (9 fl oz/1 cup) single cream
1 vanilla bean, split
6 egg yolks
120 g (4¼ oz) caster (superfine) sugar
5 g (⅛ oz) cornflour (cornstarch)
20 g (¾ oz) green-tea powder

Combine the milk and cream in a saucepan and scrape in the vanilla seeds. Bring to the boil, then remove from the heat, cover and set aside to infuse for 15 minutes.

Meanwhile, whisk the egg yolks, sugar, cornflour, green tea and a pinch of salt in a bowl until smooth. Strain the milk mixture into the egg mixture and stir well. Transfer to a clean saucepan and cook over medium heat, stirring with a wooden spoon, until the mixture coats the back of the spoon or reaches 76°C (170°F). Cool and refrigerate until chilled.

Churn the mixture in an ice-cream machine according to the manufacturer's instructions and freeze until required.

Sachima (caramelised egg fritters)

Makes 12-16

An irresistible sweet pastry, sachima is one of the most popular treats in Hong Kong and in just about all the Chinatowns around the world. Originally from Manchuria, sachima is made with strands of fried batter and coated with caramel and various other ingredients such as grated coconut, raisins and sesame seeds. This snack, also known as *ma chai*, reminds me of Rice Krispies – it's crunchy and biscuity when fresh and turns sticky and soft by the next day. It's lovely with a cup of tea or coffee. This recipe is from Dim Sum Library in Pacific Place.

200 g (7 oz) plain (all-purpose) flour
1 teaspoon bicarbonate of soda (baking soda)
2 eggs, beaten
Cornflour (cornstarch), for dusting
Vegetable oil, for deep-frying and brushing
90 g (3 oz/½ cup) roasted sesame seeds
100 g (3½ oz) caster (superfine) sugar
100 g (3½ oz) maltose

Sift the flour and bicarbonate of soda into a bowl. Add a pinch of salt and mix well. Make a well in the centre, add the eggs and mix until combined. Knead until a pliable, sticky dough forms (this can be done in a food processor fitted with the dough hook attachment). Transfer the dough to a work surface dusted with cornflour, cover and leave to rest for at least 30 minutes.

Roll out the dough to about 2 mm (1/16 inch) thick, cut into thin strips of 2–3 mm (1/16–1/8 inch) wide and dust with cornflour to prevent sticking. Heat oil in a wok or saucepan until a piece of dough rises to the surface in 20–30 seconds, then deep-fry the strips of dough in batches until light brown. Remove with a slotted spoon, drain on paper towel, then transfer to a bowl and toss with the roasted sesame seeds.

Brush a 20 x 30 cm (8 x 12 inch) baking tin with vegetable oil. Brush oil onto a piece of foil slightly larger than the tin.

Combine the caster sugar, maltose and 2½ tablespoons water in a small non-stick saucepan and bring to the boil, brushing down the side of the saucepan with a wet pastry brush. When the sugar syrup reaches 112–116°C (235–240°F) or soft-ball stage (a small teaspoon of syrup dropped into iced water forms a solid but pliable ball), quickly pour it over the fritters and toss to coat well.

Transfer the fritters to the oiled tin and flatten gently with a spatula. Lay the foil oil-side down on the fritters and roll with a rolling pin to distribute the fritters evenly. Leave to cool to room temperature, then cut into squares or rectangles. Once they're completely cool, store the fritters in an airtight container, where they'll keep for up to a week.

Basil dragon pearls, panna cotta and ginger ice cream

I fell in love with this dessert when I first dined at Yan Toh Heen, an elegant two Michelin-starred Cantonese restaurant in the InterContinental Hotel. Executive chef Lau Yiu Fai contributed this impressive recipe.

PANNA COTTA
7 g (⅛ oz) gelatine powder
200 ml (7 fl oz) milk
2 tablespoons ginger juice, squeezed
  from grated fresh ginger
40 g (1½ oz) caster (superfine) sugar
½ vanilla bean, split
200 ml (7 fl oz) single cream

BASIL DRAGON PEARLS
10 g (¼ oz) basil seeds
40 g (1½ oz) caster (superfine) sugar

CRUMBLE
15 g (½ oz) plain (all-purpose) flour
10 g (¼ oz) icing (confectioners')
  sugar
10 g (¼ oz) butter
1 teaspoon beetroot juice

SHREDDED GINGER
15 g (½ oz) julienned ginger
10 g (¼ oz) icing sugar

GINGER ICE CREAM
3 egg yolks
60 g (2¼ oz) caster (superfine) sugar
150 ml (5 fl oz) milk
2½ tablespoons single cream
40 ml (1¼ fl oz) evaporated milk
Seeds scraped from 1 vanilla bean
30 g (1 oz) ginger

GARNISH
4 longans (fresh or canned), sliced

To make the panna cotta, dissolve the gelatine in 2 tablespoons of the milk. Stir the remaining ingredients in a saucepan over medium–low heat until the sugar has dissolved. Remove from the heat, stir in the gelatine, then pour the mixture into four 125 ml (4 fl oz/½ cup) dariole moulds. Refrigerate for 5 hours until set.

To make the basil dragon pearls, soak the seeds and sugar in 2½ tablespoons water for 10–15 minutes until plump. Drain.

To make the crumble, preheat the oven to 170°C (325°F). Put all the ingredients in a bowl and rub with your fingertips until the mixture resembles fine breadcrumbs. Spread in a baking tray lined with baking paper and bake for 12–15 minutes until crisp and browned.

For the ginger, reduce the oven to 120°C (250°F). Toss the ginger and icing sugar in a bowl. Spread in a baking tin and bake for 15–20 minutes until crisp.

To make the ice cream, beat the egg yolks with 30 g (1 oz) of the sugar until pale and creamy. Put the milk, cream, evaporated milk and vanilla seeds in a saucepan and bring just to the boil. Remove from the heat and cool for 5 minutes, then, whisking constantly, whisk into the yolks. Refrigerate until chilled. Grate the ginger and strain through a fine sieve into the ice cream mixture. Stir, then churn in an ice-cream machine according to the manufacturer's instructions.

Unmould the panna cotta onto plates, garnish with shredded ginger and serve with dragon pearls, longan and scoops of ice cream on the crumble.

Ginger puddings

Serves 2

If you love the taste of ginger, this simple dessert is for you. It requires no baking or steaming and has only three ingredients: milk, sugar and ginger juice. The secret is the way the ginger reacts with heated milk, causing it to set. You need to use old fibrous ginger because it's the starch in the juice of old ginger that sets the milk. Also, unless you know your temperatures, you will need a digital kitchen thermometer. Once you add the hot milk to the ginger juice, you must leave it undisturbed. You can then eat this dessert immediately or chill it first. Said to be from the Pearl River Delta, this refreshing pudding is served at the Australia Dairy Company in Hong Kong's Yau Ma Tei district and the Yee Shun Dairy Company in Causeway Bay.

100 g (3½ oz) grated old ginger
360 ml (12¼ fl oz) milk
1 tablespoon caster (superfine) sugar, or to taste

Using a microplane or grater, grate the ginger and squeeze out the juice through muslin (cheesecloth) or a fine sieve into a bowl. You need 2 tablespoonfuls of juice. You should see a fine layer of white starch. Put 1 tablespoon of juice into each of two bowls. Heat the milk and sugar to 60–65°C (140–150°F), stirring until the sugar has dissolved.

   Stir the ginger juice, then pour the milk from a height of about 10 cm (4 inches) into the ginger juice. Don't stir and don't move the bowls. Leave for 5–10 minutes to set. Serve warm or chilled.

Walnut biscuits

Makes 25

These traditional Chinese biscuits are served during festive occasions, but also enjoyed year round. They were once made with baking ammonia and lard, but now baking powder and bicarbonate of soda have replaced the baking ammonia and, instead of lard, most recipes call for vegetable shortening or vegetable oil. This recipe for the light and extremely moreish biscuits comes courtesy of the chefs from Dim Sum Library in Pacific Place.

140 g (5 oz) raw walnut halves
300 g (10½ oz/2 cups) plain (all-purpose) flour
1 teaspoon baking powder
½ teaspoon bicarbonate of soda (baking soda)
1 egg, lightly whisked
150 ml (5½ fl oz) vegetable oil
150 g (5½ oz) caster (superfine) sugar
1 egg, beaten with 2 tablespoons water, for eggwash

Preheat the oven to 180°C (350°F) and bake the walnuts for 8 minutes or until lightly browned. Set aside 50 g (1¾ oz) and crush the remaining walnuts with a rolling pin.

Sift the flour, baking powder and bicarbonate of soda into a bowl. Mix in the crushed walnuts.

Whisk the egg, oil, sugar and a pinch of salt in a separate bowl until emulsified. Fold in the flour mixture and stir until combined.

Line baking trays with baking paper. Use your hands to roll tablespoonfuls (about 20 g/¾ oz) of walnut mixture into balls. Place the balls on the trays 5 cm (2 inches) apart, flatten lightly with a fork and press a walnut half into the centre of each. Brush with eggwash and bake for 15 minutes or until light golden.

Cool the biscuits on the trays, then store in airtight containers. They will keep for around a week.

DESSERTS AND PASTRIES

232

Vanilla soufflé

Serves 2

One of the remnants of British rule is the soufflé. At Tai Ping Koon Restaurant I once tucked into the largest soufflé I've ever seen, served in a large glass bowl and topped with twirls of overbaked meringue. The memory will remain with me forever. This version is my tribute to that soufflé.

1 tablespoon melted unsalted butter
50 g (2½ oz) caster (superfine) sugar
Ice cream, to serve

PASTRY CREAM
300 ml (10½ fl oz) milk
½ teaspoon vanilla paste or scraped seeds
    of ½ vanilla bean
4 egg yolks
40 g (1½ oz) caster (superfine) sugar
50 g (1¾ oz) cornflour (cornstarch)

MERINGUE
4 egg whites
40 g (1½ oz) caster (superfine) sugar

Preheat the oven to 200°C (400°F). Brush an ovenproof 15 cm (6 inch) glass bowl or ramekin with melted butter and dust with caster sugar, shaking out the excess (or use 2 smaller ramekins). Refrigerate to chill.

To make the pastry cream, combine the milk and vanilla paste or seeds in a saucepan and bring to the boil. Whisk the egg yolks and sugar in a bowl until light and fluffy, then mix in the cornflour.

Stir half the hot milk into the egg mixture and mix well, then add the remaining milk and stir again. Return the mixture to the saucepan and cook over medium–low heat, stirring continuously, until thickened and smooth. Transfer the pastry cream to a bowl. Cover the surface with plastic wrap and refrigerate to cool.

Transfer the cooled pastry cream to a large bowl and whisk to loosen. Set aside to return to room temperature.

To make the meringue, whisk the egg whites in a clean, dry bowl until soft peaks form. Gradually whisk in the sugar and whisk until stiff and shiny.

Gently fold one third of the meringue into the pastry cream, then fold in the remainder. Spoon into the bowl and run your thumb around the rim; this helps the soufflé to rise evenly without sticking. Bake for 12–15 minutes until well risen, then serve immediately with ice cream.

DESSERTS AND PASTRIES

234

basic recipes

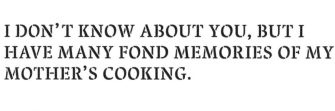

I DON'T KNOW ABOUT YOU, BUT I HAVE MANY FOND MEMORIES OF MY MOTHER'S COOKING.

One of them is the aroma of chicken stock bubbling ever so gently on the stove. It was made in an old pot that had seen the passage of time, which she filled with chicken carcasses and sometimes a few chicken feet. Along with these would be some knobbly ginger and earthy spring onions. Skimming with the ease of a trained chef – although she never was one – she removed all traces of fat and impurities to produce a clear stock of exceptional flavour. By then, the kitchen was filled with a savoury aroma that is forever locked in my consciousness.

I also have very fond memories of my mother peeling what seemed like a mountain of ginger for pickling. Harvested while still immature with tender skin, young ginger is much appreciated for its gentle flavour. It turns a shade of blushing pink when pickled and is indispensable in many Chinese dishes, including the raw fish salad that is enjoyed at Chinese New Year. It's also given as a present, along with red eggs, to celebrate a baby's one-month birthday.

Making stock and transforming the abundance of summer and autumn into an array of condiments and pickles has long been part of Chinese food tradition. Using nothing more than salt, sugar, vinegar and sometimes rice wine and soy sauce, the Chinese have been preserving an extraordinary and delicious range of food for thousands of years. Cooks such as my mother had no written recipes; instead, they relied upon oral traditions that were passed down from generation to generation. Adding a splash of nutritious stock or a soupçon of chilli oil to the most humble

ingredients to create wonderfully delicious dishes is in their DNA.

The same applies in Hong Kong. In this city of mostly Cantonese, stock-making is serious business. It's not only about sustenance and nourishment, but also about the balance of yin and yang – the guiding principle behind good Chinese cooking. It also demonstrates the skill of the cook. How the stock is made and what goes into it raises regular discussions. Just go to any wet market and you'll find cooks and housewives picking through chicken pieces or pork bones for their daily stock, as though they were jewels.

For a special occasion cooks will add a slice of air-dried Jinhua or Yunnan ham to their stock for an exquisite aroma and depth of flavour. At other times a piece of dried plaice is carefully toasted before it's used, along with pork bones, to lend depth and complexity to a wonton soup and tease jaded palates. On meat-free feast days dried shiitake mushrooms are combined with some preserved mustard greens and carrots to make the most delectable vegetarian stock. In winter some cooks add lard or schmaltz, along with collagen-rich chicken feet or pig trotters, to their stock for extra richness before turning it into hearty soups. Despite the arrival of stock cubes and MSG, Hongkongers have always shunned artificial seasoning; instead, they add a little richly concentrated stock to a stir-fry or a stew.

While stock-making forms part of the rhythm of daily life in Hong Kong, pickling and preserving are also part of the cook's routine. Most of the older generation still make their own pickles and preserves. These timeless traditions are passed on to young urban dwellers, who are not only keen to learn the art of preserving food but also, in the process, are preserving their culinary heritage. Although you might not see them drying their vegetables in the windows of residential towers in Kowloon or on Hong Kong Island, you will find them in the villages in the New Territories. Villagers with their own gardens make pickled greens along with pickled young papaya and plums. And when duck eggs are plentiful, they are brined to make salted duck eggs.

Making stock and preserving food by brining eggs or turning dried scallops into the legendary XO sauce are the essential keys to creating great Chinese food. In Hong Kong it's possible to buy just about every kind of stock, preserved food and pickle from all over China and beyond, but nothing beats the homemade variety for quality and aroma – and don't the cooks of Hong Kong know it. If you happen to be in the neighbourhood of Sheung Wan – in particular, Wing Lok Street – witness the throng of chefs and housewives sifting through the umami-rich varieties of dried seafood to be turned into the most delectable soups and great dishes.

Apart from the XO sauce, which requires a trip to your Asian supermarket for dried scallops, just about every recipe in this chapter is easy to make at home and will be rewarding in both health benefits and flavour. When you look at your freezer filled with tubs of homemade stock and your refrigerator packed with sauces and goodies you've made, you'll know you can knock up a fabulously delicious Chinese meal within minutes. And the bonus is that none of them will contain any nasty chemicals or preservatives. Chilli oil can be made within minutes and is far superior to any shop-bought variety. (In fact, some brands are even rancid and harsh with none of the subtle nuance of the homemade variety.) And once you've made your own spring onion and ginger dip – itself one of the most beautiful and addictive condiments you'll ever taste – you'll wonder why it's rarely offered in Chinese restaurants in the West.

One last thing: XO sauce is making massive inroads into the kitchens of modern Western restaurants. This seductively delicious sauce is popping up in dishes in Sydney, Melbourne, Madrid, London and New York. Its use is not solely confined to Chinese dishes. I've seen it served as a condiment with crudités, for instance, and as a sauce for pasta. So, as you can see, the recipes in this chapter are versatile and, while their souls rest firmly in the world of Chinese food, they're also delicious in Western-style meals. Go make them.

Chinese chicken stock

Makes 3 litres
(105 fl oz)

A good stock is absolutely essential for any Chinese regional cooking. This all-purpose chicken stock is not only easy to make, it lends a depth of flavour to any stir-fry or soup that just can't be achieved with a stock cube. And here's a secret: I use a mix of chicken parts – necks, wings and feet – along with carcasses to ensure the stock has a rich mouthfeel. Another tip: the mixture must be simmered over very low heat to achieve crystal-clear stock. Chinese restaurants make vast quantities of this stock and it's simmered very gently, uncovered, overnight so that the impurities remain trapped in the meat. Any scum that rises to the surface as it's simmering is skimmed off.

2 kg (4 lb 8 oz) chicken parts, such as carcasses, wings,
    necks and feet
60 g (2 oz) ginger, coarsely chopped
2 spring onions (scallions), coarsely chopped

Put the chicken parts in a large stockpot and cover with cold water. Bring to the boil, then reduce the heat and simmer for 5 minutes. Tip the chicken parts into a colander or large strainer, rinse under cold running water to remove the scum and wash out the stockpot.

Return the chicken parts to the pot, add the ginger and spring onions, cover with cold water and bring to the boil. Reduce the heat to a low simmer so the liquid is barely moving and cook, uncovered and undisturbed, for 1 hour.

Strain the stock through a fine strainer or muslin (cheesecloth) and discard the chicken parts. Cool to room temperature, then refrigerate overnight. Skim any solidified fat from the surface. The stock will keep for 3 or 4 days in the refrigerator or can be frozen in freezer bags.

BASIC RECIPES

240

Chinese superior stock

Good chicken stock is vital in Chinese cooking, but this fabulous superior stock is essential for making soups and dishes with the characteristic gelatinous quality you find in great restaurants. Exquisitely rich and absolutely clear, this is the calling card of a great chef. Cooks use a whole chicken with legs attached, pork bones, Jinhua or Yunnan ham, dried scallops and sometimes dried abalone. Jinhua ham is not available in the West, but Spanish jamón or Italian prosciutto are good substitutes. Dried scallops, sold in Asian grocers, add umami depth, but are optional. A good trick to help achieve crystal-clear stock is to soak the bones in cold water before cooking to remove the impurities.

500 g (1 lb 2 oz) pork bones
1 x 1.8 kg (4 lb) free-range chicken, quartered
    and rinsed
100 g (3½ oz) cured ham
3 dried scallops (optional)
50 g (1¾ oz) ginger, unpeeled and bruised
    with a cleaver or heavy knife
2 spring onions (scallions), trimmed
1 teaspoon whole white peppercorns
2 tablespoons rice wine

Rinse the pork bones, put in a large bowl, cover with cold water and leave to soak for 1 hour. Drain the bones, rinse well and put in a large stockpot along with the chicken. Cover with cold water, bring to the boil, then reduce the heat and simmer for 10 minutes. Tip the chicken and bones into a colander and rinse well under cold running water. Rinse the stockpot.

Put the chicken, bones and all the remaining ingredients in the stockpot and cover with plenty of cold water. Bring to the boil, then reduce the heat until the liquid is barely simmering and cook, uncovered, for at least 4 hours, skimming off any impurities that rise to the surface. Set aside to cool.

Skim any residual fat from the surface and strain the stock through a sieve lined with muslin (cheesecloth). Leave to cool completely, then refrigerate. The stock will keep refrigerated for up to a week. It can also be frozen for up to 3 months.

Chilli oil

Chilli oil is an essential ingredient in many Chinese regional cooking styles. One of the most popular brands in Hong Kong is Koon Yick Wah Kee; it's readily available in most Asian shops, although I prefer to make my own. Chilli oil is made with dried chillies and it's not difficult to prepare, but dried chillies burn easily so never cook them over high heat – once they're burnt, you have to start all over again. Just be patient and you'll be amply rewarded. I've used Sichuan dried chillies for this recipe. If you prefer a hotter chilli oil, combine them with dried bird's eye chillies or dried habaneros. Make sure you have your windows open or rangehood on, or the chilli fumes will make you cough.

100 g (3½ oz) dried red chillies (preferably Sichuan)
500 ml (17 fl oz/2 cups) sunflower oil

Snip the stems off the chillies and discard any exposed seeds. Heat a wok over low heat, add 1 teaspoon of the oil and the chillies. Stir-fry for 5–7 minutes until the chillies are fragrant and a shade darker. Transfer the chillies to a plate and leave to cool. Using a mortar and pestle, pound the chillies into coarse flakes (this can also be done in a food processor) and transfer to a heatproof bowl.

Heat the remaining oil in a wok until it begins to smoke, then immediately turn off the heat and leave to cool for 5 minutes. Pour the oil over the chilli flakes and stir carefully so it doesn't splash. Leave to cool for at least 2 hours, or preferably overnight. Strain the oil through a fine sieve into an airtight container. Chilli oil will keep for up to 2 months in the refrigerator.

Chilli sauce

This is a fresh chilli sauce from my family's kitchen. It's traditionally used with chicken rice, but is very versatile. It's delicious with steamed or grilled seafood in particular. I tend to keep the chilli seeds in because I love hot food, but remove them if you prefer a milder sauce.

6–8 large red chillies, coarsely chopped
20 g (¾ oz) ginger, peeled and sliced
4 garlic cloves, chopped
Juice of 2 limes
1 teaspoon vegetable oil

Pound the chillies, ginger, garlic and ½ teaspoon of salt with a mortar and pestle to a grainy paste. Transfer to a bowl and stir in the lime juice and oil. Can be stored for up to a week in the refrigerator.

Pickled Chinese cabbage with chilli and garlic

This simple appetiser with its sweet and sour flavours and crisp texture is a firm favourite in many Chinese families. They often make large quantities of it to ensure there is enough to last them for several days. Although two varieties of Chinese cabbage are available, the barrel-shaped, loose-headed type called wong bok or napa cabbage is preferred for this pickle. The longer cylindrical variety, wong nga pak, is often used in stir-frying. Add extra chillies if you prefer a hotter dish.

300 g (10½ oz) Chinese cabbage, leaves separated
1 tablespoon sea salt
3 tablespoons sugar
3 tablespoons rice vinegar
1 long red chilli, seeded and thinly sliced
1 garlic clove, crushed

Wash the cabbage leaves and pat dry with paper towel. Put in a bowl, add the salt, mix well and leave to stand for 1 hour.

Meanwhile, combine the sugar and rice vinegar in a small saucepan over low heat and stir until the sugar has dissolved. Remove from the heat and cool to room temperature.

Rinse the salt off the cabbage under cold running water, then drain and squeeze out the excess liquid. Thinly slice the cabbage, put in a clean bowl and add the chilli and garlic. Pour in the sugar–vinegar solution, cover and refrigerate for 2 days before using. Makes 350 g (12 oz/2 cups).

Pickled young ginger

While it's not often served in Chinese eateries in the West, pickled ginger is a fabulous appetiser offered in many restaurants and at kerb-side stalls in Hong Kong. It's enjoyed on its own or is frequently teamed with century or thousand-year eggs – delicacies that can be an acquired taste. It is also delicious in stir-fries and with roast meats. Pickled ginger is not only easy to make, it's far better than the stuff you buy in shops. Young ginger appears in summer; you can recognise it by its creamy white flesh and pinkish knobs. At a pinch, you could make this with old or mature ginger, but the tender flesh of young ginger is best.

500 g (1 lb 2 oz) young ginger, thinly sliced
    on a mandolin
250 ml (9 fl oz/1 cup) white rice vinegar
250 g (9 oz) caster (superfine) sugar

Mix the ginger and 2 tablespoons salt in a bowl and leave for 20 minutes. Transfer the ginger to a colander and rinse under cold running water. Pat dry with paper towel and set it aside in a heatproof bowl.

Put the rice vinegar, sugar, 1 teaspoon salt and 125 ml (4 fl oz/½ cup) water in a saucepan. Bring to a simmer, stirring until the sugar has dissolved.

Pour the vinegar–sugar solution over the ginger, ensuring the ginger is completely covered (it will turn a creamy pink colour within 5 minutes). Cover the bowl, cool to room temperature, then refrigerate for 1 week to pickle. Pickled young ginger can be kept in the refrigerator for 1 month.

Note *Buy a couple of century eggs from an Asian supermarket and serve them sliced with this ginger. Century eggs are duck or quail eggs preserved in a mixture of rice husks, lime, ash and salt. Properly cured, the whites are wobbly and golden brown and the yolks a creamy green with a distinctive smell of mature cheese. One of the best places to enjoy this delicacy is at the legendary Yung Kee restaurant in Hong Kong.*

Cantonese spring onion and ginger dip

Makes 750 ml
(26 fl oz/
3 cups)

This easy-to-make classic Cantonese dip is a treat. It's fresh, aromatic and addictive, and is particularly good with poached chicken and steamed seafood. I also use it as a dip with savoury pastries such as spring onion pancakes and dumplings.

200 g (7 oz) ginger, peeled and chopped
5 spring onions (scallions), chopped
1 teaspoon sugar, or to taste
250 ml (9 fl oz/1 cup) vegetable oil

Combine all the ingredients and a pinch of salt in a food processor and blend until smooth. Taste and adjust the seasoning. This dip can be kept in the refrigerator for 3 to 4 days.

Salted duck eggs

Makes 12

Salted duck eggs have been around for centuries. Wonderfully versatile, these brined eggs are great with rice or congee, or used to flavour stir-fried bitter gourd and prawns. One of the most innovative uses for these eggs is in a sweet dim sum called lava bao. While other eggs can be used for brining, duck eggs are best because of their fat content – good ones should have a film of oil around the yolk when cooked. Chopped salted duck egg is also delicious on steamed greens such as Chinese broccoli and asparagus.

12 duck eggs, wiped clean
315 g (11¼ oz/1 cup) rock salt

Put the duck eggs in a sterilised jar. Put the salt and 1 litre (35 fl oz/4 cups) water in a saucepan and bring to the boil, stirring until the salt has dissolved. Remove from the heat and cool to room temperature.

Pour the cooled brine solution over the eggs. Put a small plate on top to keep them submerged, seal the jar and leave in a cool place to pickle. After 30 days, test whether they're ready by boiling an egg for 6 minutes. If it's salty enough for your taste, they're ready; otherwise leave the eggs for another 10 days.

Once the eggs are ready, remove them from the brining solution and store them in the refrigerator for up to 2 weeks. To serve, boil the eggs for 6 minutes.

XO sauce

Created in Hong Kong in the 1980s, this condiment quickly became a favourite among the cognoscenti who graced the fine dining rooms of the city's élite restaurants. Named after XO Cognac, it's undoubtedly one of the most luxurious of Chinese sauces, made with expensive ingredients such as conpoy, or dried scallop, which costs around $A600 per kilo, and the fabled dry-aged ham from Yunnan. It's exotic and addictive.

While the origins of XO sauce are hazy, most of the chefs and restaurateurs I've spoken to believe it came from Spring Moon, the Cantonese restaurant in the grand Peninsula hotel. And in my notes for a piece I wrote in the 1990s, the restaurant told me their chefs have been making this sauce since 1986.

So what does this legendary sauce taste like? The first thing that hits you is the umami of the conpoy and ham. The shallots and chillies that have infused the proteins then create a gorgeous tingling sensation on the palate.

While the best XO sauce can be savoured on its own, it's marvellous with dumplings or a plate of stir-fried greens. It's also excellent with braised egg noodles and as a topping on bean curd or steamed rice.

The traditional method for making this sauce is to deep-fry the shredded scallops, but my shallow-fried version works a treat. The quantity I've given is large but can be halved. Use smoked bacon if jamón is not available, and start the recipe a day in advance to rehydrate the dried scallops and shrimp.

100 g (3½ oz) dried scallops, rinsed
30 g (1 oz) dried shrimp, rinsed
30 g (1 oz) dried red chillies, soaked
   in hot water for 30 minutes
500 ml (17 fl oz/2 cups) vegetable
   oil, plus extra for storing
150 g (5½ oz) garlic, finely chopped
150 g (5½ oz) red Asian shallots,
   finely chopped

20 g (¾ oz) ginger, finely chopped
150 g (5½ oz) long red chillies,
   seeded and finely chopped
200 g (7 oz) jamón, finely chopped
15 g (½ oz) dried shrimp roe
   (optional)
Sugar, to taste

Put the scallops and shrimp in separate containers, cover with warm water and leave to soak overnight.

Drain the scallops, reserving the soaking water, into a bowl and shred the scallops with your fingers to separate the fibres. Drain the dried shrimp, reserving the soaking water, and finely chop. Set both aside.

Drain the softened dried chillies and pound or grind to a coarse paste.

Heat the oil in a wok over high heat, then reduce the heat to medium. Add the garlic, shallots and ginger and stir-fry for 5 minutes until fragrant. Add the dried and fresh chillies and stir-fry for 2–3 minutes until fragrant. Add the scallops, shrimp and jamón and stir-fry gently for another 5 minutes. Add the reserved soaking liquid and stir well. Cook for 20–30 minutes over medium–low heat, stirring occasionally, until the liquid has evaporated.

Add the shrimp roe, if using, and season with sugar and salt to taste. Cool, place in jars, cover with oil and store in the refrigerator for a month or so, topping up the oil occasionally.

index

Thank you

Murdoch Books; in particular, Lou Johnson, Corinne Roberts, Jane Price, Vivien Valk, Madeleine Kane and my friend Sue Hines. Thank you also to my many friends and family for your support during my time in Hong Kong and Australia. My gratitude to Michael and Janet Tan, the Nolascos, the Connollys, the Tighes, Shaun Campbell, Evelyn Yo, Vivienne Gan, Daniel Cheong, Alka Datwani, Janice Leung Hayes, Mina Park, Earl Carter, Greg Elms, Caroline Velik, Patrick Trovato, Charmaine Mok, Pat Nourse, Lisa Featherby, Toni Mason, Amy Powell, Mimi Cheung, Janene Ferguson, Philip Yu, Gladis Young, Shane Osborn, Richard Ekkebus, Eddie McDougall, Carole Klein, Miryana Power, Paul Hicks, Angela Li, Jowett Yu, May Chow, Kee Foong, Vivian Li, Denny Ip, Jason and Cindy Lui, Peggy Chan, Troy Wheeler and Chui Lee Luk.

My appreciation also goes to the Hong Kong Tourism Board, Langham, Peninsula, Mandarin Oriental, Ritz-Carlton, Grand Hyatt, InterContinental, Four Seasons, East and Icon hotels. Finally, to my parents who taught me how to cook and love good food.

Published in 2017 by Murdoch Books, an imprint of Allen & Unwin

Murdoch Books Australia
83 Alexander Street,
Crows Nest NSW 2065
Phone: +61 (0)2 8425 0100
murdochbooks.com.au
info@murdochbooks.com.au

Murdoch Books UK
Ormond House, 26–27 Boswell Street,
London WC1N 3JZ
Phone: +44 (0) 20 8785 5995
murdochbooks.co.uk
info@murdochbooks.co.uk

For corporate orders and custom publishing contact our business development team at salesenquiries@murdochbooks.com.au

Publisher: Corinne Roberts
Design Manager: Vivien Valk
Editorial Manager: Jane Price
Designer: Madeleine Kane
Photographer: Greg Elms
Stylist: Caroline Velik
Production Manager: Lou Playfair

Text © Tony Tan 2017
Design © Murdoch Books 2017
Photography © Greg Elms 2017

ISBN 978 1 76052 269 8 Australia
ISBN 978 1 76052 771 6 UK
A cataloguing-in-publication entry is available from the catalogue of the National Library of Australia at nla.gov.au
A catalogue record for this book is available from the British Library

Colour reproduction by Splitting Image Colour Studio Pty Ltd, Clayton, Victoria
Printed by C & C Offset Printing, China

Measures guide We have used 20 ml (4 teaspoon) Australian tablespoon measures. If you are using a 15 ml (3 teaspoon) tablespoon, add an extra teaspoon of the ingredient for each tablespoon specified.

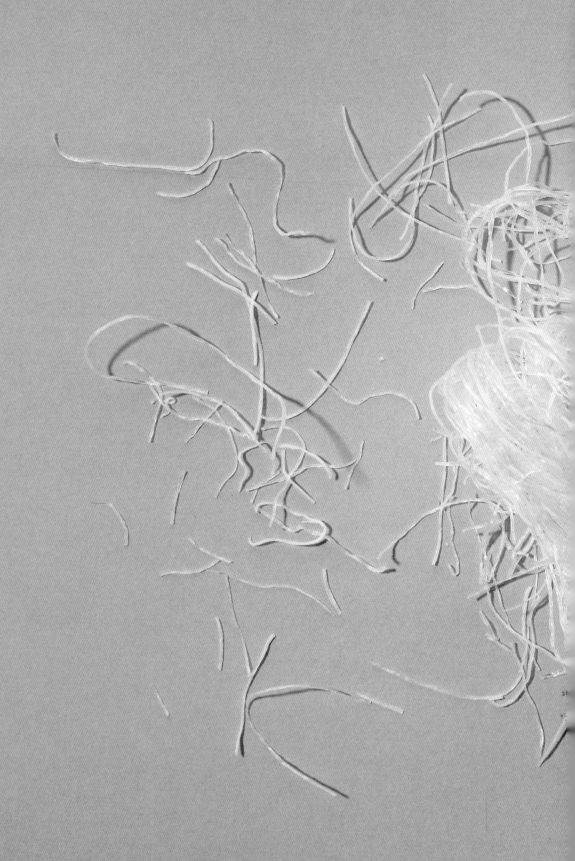